The Ghetto Swinger
Coco Schumann

The Ghetto Swinger

A BERLIN JAZZ-LEGEND REMEMBERS

COCO SCHUMANN

WITH

Max Christian Graeff and Michaela Haas

TRANSLATION

John Howard

AFTERWORD

Michael H. Kater

The Ghetto Swinger

A BERLIN JAZZ-LEGEND REMEMBERS

Coco Schumann

WITH Max Christian Graeff and Michaela Haas
© 1997 Deutscher Taschenbuch Verlag GmbH & Co. KG, Munich/Germany

TRANSLATION John Howard

AFTERWORD Michael H. Kater

ENGLISH TRANSLATION © 2016 DoppelHouse Press, Los Angeles

BOOK DESIGN Curt Carpenter

Photographs from the archive of Coco Schumann, unless otherwise noted.
TITLE PAGE: Coco Schumann, 2014. PHOTO: Susann Welscher

Publisher's Cataloging-in-Publication data
NAMES: Schumann, Coco, 1924-, author. | Graeff, Max Christian, contributor. | Haas, Michaela, 1970-, contributor | Howard, John, 1942-, translator. | Kater, Michael H., 1937-, afterword author.
TITLE: The Ghetto Swinger : a Berlin Jazz Legend Remembers / Coco Schumann ; with Max Christian Graeff and Michaela Haas ; translation [by] John Howard ; afterword [by] Michael H. Kater.
DESCRIPTION: Los Angeles, CA: Dopplehouse Press, 2016.
IDENTIFIERS: ISBN 978-0-9832540-4-1 (Hardcover) | 978-0-9987770-6-1 (pbk.) 978-0-9832540-6-5 (ebook) | LCCN 2015948459
SUBJECTS: LCSH Schumann, Coco, 1924-. | Jazz musicians--Germany--Biography. | Swing (Music)--Germany. | Guitarists--Germany--Biography. | Jews--Germany--Biography. | World War, 1939-1945--Personal narratives, Jewish.
BISAC BIOGRAPHY & AUTOBIOGRAPHY / Music
BIOGRAPHY & AUTOBIOGRAPHY / Historical
BIOGRAPHY & AUTOBIOGRAPHY / Jewish
CLASSIFICATION: LCC ML419.S33 A3 2016 | DDC 787.87/165/09–dc23

 Doppelhouse Press
LOS ANGELES, CALIFORNIA

CONTENTS

If I hadn't been six-foot five, blond and Germanic,
I never would have made it through all this.

Author's Preface

I HAVE PLAYED GUITAR and percussion since I was thirteen years old. At the beginning of the 1940s, I played as a guitarist in many clubs in Berlin. At the time, I was a star in the Berlin swing scene, even when the Nazis banned this music. No one knew that I was Jewish. It was forbidden for Jews to play music and to have contact with Aryan Germans. It was mandatory to wear the yellow Star of David. I did not adhere to these prohibitions and obligations, and I was betrayed. At the age of nineteen, in 1943, I was deported to Theresienstadt ghetto, and at twenty, I was sent to the concentration camp in Auschwitz-Birkenau. In this book, I tell you how music saved my life.

The camps and the fear changed my life, but the music has kept me going, and has made everything good again. I have survived. I am a musician who spent time in concentration camps, not someone in a concentration camp who also played a little music.

It was much later, in the mid-1980s, that I began to talk about my time in Theresienstadt and Auschwitz-Birkenau in films, in the media and in schools. As a young person, I could not believe what some people were capable of inflicting on others. I have learned that we must never allow ourselves to bend based on others' views. What matters is one's own convictions and mutual respect, regardless of race, color, religion and political points of view.

In 1997, my book "The Ghetto Swinger" was published, which is now being published in English. I am very happy about this.

Coco Schumann
BERLIN, MARCH 2015

Me on the left in front of the Gedächtniskirche in Berlin, circa 1942, with my friend, the pianist Herbert Giesler. Against regulations, I have my Star of David in my pocket. The scratches on the photo remain a mystery.

How High the Moon

T HE FINAL NOTES of *How High the Moon* fade away. A warm night in August. After the applause dies, I put my old Gibson guitar to one side, step to the front door of the nightclub, the *Ewige Lampe* (Eternal Lamp), and look up at the sky above Charlottenburg. The moon sits high over the houses and beams down on me this evening, mirroring my own worries. It's gotten very late again – is this proper for a man my age? I asked myself this question sixty years ago when I was a twelve-year-old who loved to party the nights away. The major part of my life spanned those two points in time. A picture of me was published in a popular newspaper with the words *Coco Schumann: The Terrible Life of a Jazz Legend!* But it was not true. No, my dear fellow, I tell myself facing the bright moon; it was wild and flamboyant, sometimes too long and always too short, but life has turned out both unbelievably evil and so beautiful it takes your breath away. However, one thing it certainly never was: terrible.

The reporter who wrote those words did not intend to be cruel; quite the opposite. Those words reflect one of the misunderstandings that popped up when I told the story of my life – because there were a few years that didn't just change me, they changed the world. I am a child of my times and as such, being also Jewish, I spent a few years in a Nazi concentration camp, like millions of other people. My life could easily have come to an early, very sudden end. For a brief period that seemed to go on forever, I couldn't be sure there would be a tomorrow. I am grateful right up to this day that tomorrow did come, that it kept coming until the danger passed. This feeling of gratitude has never left me. Unlike millions of others, I survived. I didn't want to talk about it and was not able to – until forty years after the fact.

Berlin Air

OUR TEACHER had asked each of us to bring five pennies to school. A couple of days later we stepped into the classroom with our pennies in our pockets. A large rhomboid-shaped board with holes drilled into it was leaning against the blackboard. We lined up in rows and waited quietly. One after another, my classmates "bought" a nail with their pennies, a nail that had a big brass head. They stepped up to the board and nailed it into one of the holes in the board. Our teacher explained that what was taking shape here before our eyes – with every one of us making a contribution – was a new alliance, the Hitler Youth, and that all of us were now fellow members. All of us, I thought – until it was my turn. When I went up to buy my nail, the teacher stopped me. In front of the whole class, he told me I was a Jew and that Jews could not join. I stared at him but did not understand, went back to my desk and sat down. It was the first time somebody had told me that I was a Jew and that I was not what I thought I was – a German, a friend, a part of what was going on in my country.

After school, I slouched home, devastated. At first I thought the teacher was mad at me because of a joke I had once played on him. He had tried to create a good atmosphere in the classroom by announcing he would only shop at our parents' businesses. I told him to be sure to shop at my mom's place. The joke was that he was bald and did not know my mom owned a hair salon! That evening my parents explained very carefully what these new times were all about. I was too young to understand – or maybe I did not want to understand. At first I just thought the teacher had it in for me, but my classmates soon "helped" me comprehend the situation. I had gotten along with them just fine before, but now they insisted on a previously unknown difference between them and me.

If I remember correctly, May 14, 1924 was a calm, sunny day. Germans were keeping their eyes on events as they unfolded after the election of the second parliament in Weimar Germany. The electorate was divided into two camps – German Nationalists vs. National Socialists. Even the Communists had done well. The Democrats and the other middle-of-the-road parties had lost most of their seats. During the rampant inflation of the Weimar Republic, the last bundles of cash were used to make toy mountains in the playrooms of children. Now you could buy pig knuckles for fourteen cents a pound instead of having to pay millions as the value of your money fell by the hour. In Paris, the French completed the last preparations for the VIII Olympics, while all of Italy mourned the sudden death of actress Eleonora Duse. In Berlin, the in-crowd went mad for the mass media of the future, and they spent a lot of time sitting around a radio set listening to popular music. It would be a long time, though, before every home would have a radio. People would go to their favorite hangout every Wednesday to listen to their favorite orchestra, to escape the political stuff and to sing along to Louis Armstrong lyrics like *I wish I could shimmy like my sister Kate!* – or, adapted to the Berlin dialect: *When you shimmy, when you dance the blues, you step on my shoes!* Meanwhile, in a prison in Landsberg, Bavaria, an inmate named Adolf Hitler dictated the first chapter of a book he called *Mein Kampf*.

None of that mattered to me this first evening of my life. What mattered was how to make my way in this world. Thrilled, an untold number of my aunts welcomed yours truly, Heinz Jakob Schumann, as they sighed and passed me around.

My mom, Hedwig, born Rothholz, a German Jew, was a beautician – like most of her seven siblings. She worked in the hair salon of her father, Louis Rothholz, in the Scheunenviertel, the Barnyard Quarter of Berlin. We lived on Gormannstrasse, near the Rosenthaler Platz. My dad, Alfred, who came from a Thuringian family of craftsmen, was an interior decorator, an upholsterer and what would later be called an "Aryan". We lived quite simply, modestly, content – like typical Germans. Dad was patriotic to a fault. He was proud that he had been wounded several times fighting on the front lines during World War I. The only one who could trump that was my Jewish grandfather, who wore a magnificent Kaiser Wilhelm beard. He decorated his living room with helmets and swords and was always happy when I stood in awe in front of his ensemble of mementoes while listening reverently to his exuberant stories.

Our family did not distinguish itself by their religious ardor. The Christian branch of the family got along well with the Jewish branch. The back and forth of both religions did not pose any problems. On the contrary, we were happy

The basement hair salon of my grandfather Louis Rothholz
located on the Elsässer Strasse (now Torstrasse)

about the prospect of enriching our everyday life by celebrating Jewish holidays. The Christmas tree stood next to the Chanukah candles; Easter was celebrated with my father's parents, Passover at my mother's family. My family did not see much difference between the two religions, something I thought was ideal at the time. My entire childhood was spent that way – unencumbered and carefree.

My dad, who had joined the Jewish Community when he married my mom, had a *mohel* circumcise me a few days after my birth, and with that – something nobody even bothered to discuss – I became a "second-class halfbreed".

My dad insisted that I go with him to the temple in the Oranienburger Strasse. The atmosphere of the Jewish community in the center of Berlin was certainly formative and I only need to close my eyes to see it all again, so it remains familiar to me and a pleasant memory. I have not been able to recall any concrete events from the religious life of my childhood. Street life fascinated me more than life in the Jewish community – even when I was little – and I was more interested in the culinary delights, the relaxed atmosphere and the music than the reason for any celebration. I enjoyed the Jewish holidays when I was excused from class, even though I attended a Lutheran School regularly, and I could run around the Barnyard Quarter of Berlin all I wanted.

In addition to hanging out, I had only one other favorite thing when I was young – music. All of my relatives were more or less musically inclined, and they sang or played an instrument. My parents were the exception. They could play the gramophone brilliantly and devoured everything those fast times offered.

True Berliners, they listened to Paul Lincke's songs a hundred times each, like his arrangement of *Glow Little Glow Worm*, as well as the modern versions of these "loud, turbulent days": revues, American film music, the foxtrot, the Charleston, jazz and black bottoms. "Tempo" was a word that was bandied about a lot, the world of music stood on its head. There was a new hit every day and new renditions, old chestnuts were "jazzed up", and someone even tried to take the old marching song, *Berlin Air*, and syncopate its rhythm. On the classical side of the musical spectrum, the tenor Richard Tauber cancelled his opera engagements to become the lead singer in Franz Lehár's operettas. The first radio set you could listen to without wearing a headset, one that had an amplifier and a loudspeaker, was soon in German living rooms and added a certain bounce to life.

Every day when my mom and dad would leave the house, I would pull up a chair in front of the radio set, take two large soup spoons and drum on the table every way I could get my hands and arms to move. Or, to the horror of my neighbors, I would grab an accordion someone had thoughtlessly given me after Aunt Trudy's husband let me play his bandoneón. What I loved to do on Sunday morning was to pretend to be the star accordion player of the Dajos Béla dance orchestra in the Hotel Adlon. Making all sorts of daring movements while I played, I accompanied songs on the radio like *Broadway Melody*, *Constantinople* or the Kálmán hit *Im Himmel spielt auch schon die Jazzband* (The Jazz Band Is Already Playing in Heaven). Initially, my captive audience enjoyed my performance. After a few bars, it got on their nerves.

My favorite uncle, Arthur, the brother of my mom and of course a hairdresser, played drums for a gypsy band in the Berlin Prater, the famous outdoor amusement park. I still have vivid memories of the morning after a birthday party at my grandmother's where the band had played. I must have been four years old. I was the first one to get up and admire the instruments that were lying around, sat down at my uncle's drum set and let it rip. This did not fail to produce an effect, as much with regards to my sleeping surroundings as with my future. I knew from that moment on I wanted to be a musician. Music was like a virus I would live with for the rest of my life.

As nice as it was at home, I spent much more of my childhood playing in the street than in the living room. My parents were out most of the day, even when my dad joined the swelling ranks of the unemployed. He was always going somewhere to take on all kinds of odd jobs. One of the most touching images of those days was the view from our window down to the unemployment office, to

In the courtyard of Uncle Arthur, my first day at school, 1929

the gray, endless lines of people looking for work. The general mood was like the political landscape in Germany: marked by extremes. Gloomy oppression on the one hand and irrational exuberance and improvisation on the other.

We had to think of something if we wanted to survive. My mom kept us going by making house calls to her regular customers and had to go to every suburb in Berlin. Her brother, Arthur, was a Jack-of-all-trades and pretty typical for the Barnyard Quarter. He knew even then how to take advantage of any opportunity that presented itself, and his business flourished. I can still see him standing in front of me, in front of the large mirror, together with Uncle Max. They had drawn a moustache on their faces with an eyeliner pencil, wore a straw hat we used to call a boater, wore Knickerbockers and furiously practiced the Charleston while playing the latest records. I think Uncle Arthur impressed

With my mother Hedwig Schumann, born Rothholz, and my father Alfred, no date

me more than anyone else in my family and was a huge influence. He always appeared at our family parties in a tuxedo wearing a white chrysanthemum in his lapel. He was a man of the world; he went to all the balls one had to go to and played in many bands.

I only discovered the most exciting part of the Barnyard Quarter after we had moved out. We lived in Rudow for a while, and later, on Kottbusser Damm, where my mom worked around the clock at her own hair salon on the basement level, which she was able to rent for a good price. I had to make my own way early on in life and tried to organize my days in a useful way. Most of the time I would start off in my mother's shop by striking up a conversation with her customers and got on everyone's nerves so much that they gave me a few pennies to get rid of me. Then I would go pester the relatives who lived in Berlin Mitte.

The Barnyard Quarter had a prickly atmosphere for roaming around. It was a poor but lively place where everyone had to see how he would get through the day. We Jews called the district "Dark Medina" after the Arab word for city or district, medina; it was not exactly a posh part of town. There was not much left of the wooden barns and cow stalls built there in the 17th century. Since the turn of the 20th century, Hasidic Jews, who had been driven from the *shtetls* of the East to the Prussian metropolis by anti-Semitic bigotry, had enriched everyday life. Originally their plan had been to immigrate to the coast and then to America, but several thousand of them decided to stay in the Berlin Mitte and make their own little Galicia around the Barnyard Quarter.

The *Mulackei*, named after the notorious Mulackstrasse that branched off from the Gormannstrasse, was home to the demimonde and underworld of Berlin. The scene the Berliners unmistakably called *das Milljoeh*, the milieu, developed rapidly. When I was a small boy I had asked myself why so many ladies stood around all night long in front of apartment buildings, but since I kept my eyes open it was easy to figure out. I hung out in the streets between our old apartment and the Alexanderplatz and watched the day-to-day comings and goings, the prostitutes, the underworld, the poor broken hustlers who belonged to gangs like the *Ringverein* (The Wrestling Club). The members of this criminal association dressed more elegantly. The haberdasher shops in the area profited from these gentlemen's tastes, and the barbers did well, too. I did okay talking the ears off my relatives one after the other and collecting the pennies they gave me to leave them alone.

Uncle Willie had a livery stable with horse-drawn coaches on Linienstrasse just opposite of Uncle Arthur's shop. In the inner courtyard of a block of buildings was a stable with horses and a few cows. There was a dairy there and a butcher shop. I went there to get sausage soup for my aunts that was left-over from making blood and liver sausages. It tasted wonderful. If I ever looked inside the soup jug to see what curious things were floating around inside, I was told: "You'll eat what the ladle provides!" We never really ate kosher. Too many kinds of culinary improvisations were available to us. I acquired a taste from those days for simple, artful meals, which has stayed with me all these years. My mom and my aunts had the gift of conjuring up the most stupendous meals from little or nothing. They always had an old "Swedish recipe" someone had given to them.

Special dishes were served, however, on Jewish holidays. When I came home from the temple with my grandfather, my dad, my Uncle Arthur and Uncle Max, milk coffee was served with crumbled matzo bread, my favorite dish; for supper they served mazzo cinnamon dumplings made with sugar and almonds that were boiled in chicken broth. I will always associate this dish with Seder evenings, and the first two evenings of Passover, the one holiday where I, as the youngest at the table, had to recite a Hebrew prayer I had learned by heart. To be perfectly honest, I could only recite it phonetically: *Ma nischtana haLaila hazeh michal haLeilot . . .* It's in the Passover Haggadah and is one of the four questions for the youngest child: "Why is this night different from all other nights?" The fact that we could not eat before I had finally spoken these words added suspense to the ritual and somehow managed to combine effort with pleasure. In this regard we were rather casual about the whole thing, nobody was forced to really deal with it. It was only after 1933 that others explained to me I was a Jew and what that presumably meant.

I experienced the National Socialists' takeover in January 1933 as a torchlight parade across the Kottbusser Damm. I was already familiar with the brown uniforms, but as an eight-year-old boy I did not ask any questions about everyday things that were considered "normal". This parade changed that. It did not feel threatening, but the thrust of the uniforms and the power of the image that was presented fascinated me. The gloomy splendor of this theatrical performance captivated my heart, just as it did with most other Germans. Those who were marching were the ones who wanted to make a better world out of the bad times we lived in now, so they said. As a child I felt just as German as my Catholic or Protestant schoolmates. For me, there was no difference between us. Until the day we each had to bring five pennies to school.

One day, two members of the SA (*Sturm Abteilung*, aka Brownshirts) stood in front of my mother's shop, painted the Star of David on her shop window and stopped her customers from entering. It was the same sight all over the city, with fights, beatings and arrests. The police joined the SA troops; the blood of "provocative" Jews and members of the opposition was flowing in the streets. My mom began to receive regular visits from the SA. Finally, in 1934, my dad decided to move to Halensee, a posh district at the end of Kurfürstendamm, to avoid these visits. Nobody there knew that my mom was a Jew. We rented a large five-bedroom apartment that was quite cheap because some windows opened towards railroad tracks. My mom soon opened another hair salon, which quickly took off. I went to a nearby school; my classmates did not suspect a thing. Everyday life returned to normal for the moment.

That is, until my new teacher got wind of me and began to make cutting remarks. After that, most of my schoolmates gave me a hard time, but I had resolved out of a combination of incomprehension and stubbornness to ignore their taunts. I had no quarrel with the new regime; on the contrary, I wanted to participate in what was going on – whatever it was. The attempt to close down my mother's beauty salon that forced us to move was forgotten so I did not have to draw any conclusions from it. Anyway, I knew plenty of people who wanted to be my friend. I had no idea the official persecution of Jews would begin with the enactment of the Nuremberg Laws in September of 1935.

By October, as the "Law to Protect the Inheritable Traits of the German People" was enacted, with its evidence of Aryan ancestry and its marriage restrictions, my dad was once again forced to make a decision which was easy for him, and that is why I will always believe my dad was a hero. Not because of brave actions on behalf of his German fatherland, but because he gave a clear answer to a clear question. The National Socialists had advised him earlier to correct his "mistake", to get a divorce from his wife to save his "Aryan" skin. But even now after the Nuremberg Laws required him to give a definitive answer, this courageous man didn't hesitate a second to say: "I am not going to abandon my family!" It is not my style to admire things or deeds but here I make an exception, even though I would only be able to gauge the risk he was taking many years later.

School did not offer much of anything that interested me. I was in the lower rung in everything but sports and music. Our music teacher began to show some understanding for my poor showing in the other subject he taught me, math. He took me aside one day and said: "Don't worry about it, you're a musician after all." Some of my friends had instruments and began to get together to play jazz in their homes.

I was roving about. I had extended my radius for hanging out significantly after moving into the new apartment. As before, I visited our relatives in the center of town, collected my pennies, earned some extra money by helping out at a fruit dealer's shop at the Lehniner Platz and managed to save up a nice sum while my parents were earning less and less. I invested it at a Weba ice cream shop, which had the biggest ice cream sandwiches in all of Berlin. It was located in the Charlottenburg Pestalozzistrasse, directly across from the apartment of my grandparents on my father's side.

Clubs on the Friedrichstrasse at night, Berlin, 1930
COURTESY: DEUTSCHE FOTOTHEK

Jazz venue *Haus Vaterland*
COURTESY: BUNDESARCHIV

Weintraub's Syncopators, March 28, 1929
PHOTO: JOSEF SCHMIDT | COURTESY: DEUTSCHES HISTORISCHES MUSEUM, BERLIN

A couple of boys, a little older than I, hung out at a lot next to the ice cream shop. They gave me some lip, I gave some back, we fought, I handed a knuckle sandwich to a couple of them and was accepted as a member in good standing. It was my first encounter with "The Swings" in early 1936.

From then on we met daily, rode our bicycles to the countryside around Berlin or went swimming in the lake. Most of the time we hung out at the Weba ice cream shop and listened to records. One of us worked at the post office, and we called him the "postal inspector". He was already earning some money and could afford to dress "English". Long jackets were the cool thing, pointed collars, and thin ties tied with a very small knot we called a dipsy doodle. The "postal inspector" had what looked like a briefcase with him at all times, which was actually a portable leather-clad Telefunken record player. Within a week I could dig the music my friends played. We had the coolest, latest records: Duke Ellington, the Chick Webb Band with the recently-discovered Ella Fitzgerald, Horst Winter, Teddy Stauffer, Nat Gonella, the Golden Seven with Kurt Hohenberger on trumpet, and, if I remember correctly, we even had Artie Shaw's *Japanese Sandman*. They were well stocked. Coincidence – or perhaps it was instinct or an unconscious impression made by the lively variations of music – put me in the path of people who changed the course of my life forever in a couple of days. From this time on, my life was devoted to jazz and swing.

In 1936 the nights of Berlin were ablaze. For one thing, the National Socialist regime had taken over every aspect of government and showed its true face; on the other hand, Berlin was infected by an "un-German" fever called swing. Starting in 1930, the Nazis tried to stamp out this "Anglo-Jewish infestation", as they called it. Their actions led to an exodus of popular celebrity musicians: Dajos Béla left for Holland in 1933 before he finally settled in Argentina in 1936. The magnificent Weintraub's Syncopators emigrated to Australia while touring. Their former pianists Friedrich Hollaender and Franz Wachsmann took off for the United States where Wachsmann became one of the most sought-after film composers in Hollywood. Another former pianist of the Syncopators, Martin Roman, settled in Holland. Oddly enough, we did not develop a political awareness despite these and many other losses to German music. We still had an enormous freedom to play because the definitions of what was permissible or not remained flexible, and the dynamics of events completely overwhelmed the watchdogs of virtue and morality.

Unlike literature and art, composers, musicians and interpreters were not so easy to keep out of the public realm and prevent from doing their jobs. The regime could not do without broad sectors of the "entertainment industry" from one moment to the next. As early as 1933, the *Reichsmusikkammer* (Reich's Music Chamber – a national association of musicians) prohibited the use of "foreign or foreign-sounding pseudonyms". The Hadamovsky Decree in October of 1935 prohibited playing "nigger jazz" on air, but this decree proved impossible to enforce. The fans tuned into foreign stations and record imports were booming. Berlin was already wired when the decrees were relaxed further as the 1936 Olympics drew near. The Nazis wanted to show the world what a spectacular country they were in the process of creating; how they controlled matters and how they had incorporated them into their own entertainment.

Swing and jazz in all of its variations were considered to be part of the presumably harmful excesses of life. But the decree ran head-on into the problems presented when trying to enforce it, and the obvious entertainment value of this music resulted in a somewhat strange and contradictory acceptance. Those in power decided to use the momentum of this music for the time being, as the eyes of the world were on the Olympic city of Berlin, a city that would shine in all its splendor. Who could know that while the games were happening, the concentration camp Sachsenhausen was nearing completion on the outskirts of Berlin?

You Can't Stop Me
from Dreaming

THERE WAS SOMETHING about springtime evenings that beckoned me to the brightly-lit streets around the Kurfürstendamm with its rows of hangouts, cafés and bars, one next to the other. Bands were playing in all of them. I slipped from door to door listening to the muffled tones and music fragments and inhaled the aroma of that big, wide world whirling out of the ventilators above the entrances; the elusive fragrance of perfume, smoke and alcohol filled my nostrils, and after some time I tried to figure out the names of the bands and the titles of the songs they were playing.

The legendary *Delphi-Palast* was an extraordinary place, a Mecca for everyone who loved swing. After being closed for a long time, Josef König, a Jewish restaurateur, reopened it in 1930 with extravagant appointments – receding roof, hydraulic stages in the dance floor, and table telephones. He became a legend almost instantly, but by 1936 he had emigrated. However, his lady friend and his son kept the *Delphi* open during the year of the Olympics and watched it flourish. This is where that memorable guest appearance of the great Teddy Stauffer took place, with his original Teddies, who had only been allowed to keep their "English" names with a special permit from the Reichskulturkammer. Two weeks after Stauffer had arrived and two weeks before the opening of the Olympic Games on August 1, 1936, against all the laws to the contrary, he recorded his first album for Telefunken with *Goody, Goody for Me* and *Alone,* right under the eyes of the wavering dictatorship which was peering at the hard cash from the international visitors. As he said later, it was "the greatest hit in the history of Germany up to that time". In the same year Telefunken released at least ten more records, all of them international hits by Jewish composers and songwriters.

At thirteen years old, I sat on the wall that encircled the spacious front garden of the *Delphi* and observed the proceedings. The dancers bobbed on the dance floor under the stars through the warm summer nights, and the waiters had to perform their own elegant contortions to serve the crowded tables. Stauffer's band unleashed a torrent of pure enthusiasm with its caprioles and antics. I listened to each and every one of those notes and wanted nothing more than to be part of that world. At least as a paying member of the audience, as an elegant dancer – as a grown-up, not as an onlooker. The bands began to play in the afternoon and did not stop until late at night. An exciting mix of celebrities was present: in addition to Stauffer, Max Rumpf, Günther Herzog, Heinz Weber and many others played at the *Delphi*.

When I would slip into our apartment late at night, my poor frazzled mom would be waiting for me. She would slap me up alongside the head out of worry. She must have been terribly concerned about me, which was more than understandable in those times. I could not help her with her worries for the time being. From now on, there was no going back!

During the following year things got worse. It was hard to find any good swing records. The "Prohibition of non-Aryan art and music" began to affect numerous musicians. Benny Goodman was a prominent example. After the Nazis discovered the Jew in him and his blessed hands had mutated into "criminal hands" from one day to the other, his records vanished from the programs of German companies. Now we depended on imported records and on those that many German swing fans brought with them from neighboring countries. We would find them a short while later being sold by a peddler, where the records had wound up due to a sudden fit of nationalistic fervor or a bad conscience. Otherwise, we would have needed a lot of money to get hold of them – and that is what we did not have. It did not put a dent in our enthusiasm though; a few of us could already play pretty well.

We grew up fast in those days, or a better way to put it would be to say we looked older faster in those days. I was only thirteen, but I looked two or three years older and wanted to feel as old as I looked. I would stroll down the street after school with a classmates whose parents were well off and who had a steady supply of cigarettes "available". We stuck them in our faces, tried to look important and said things like, "Fine weed, fine weed!"

It must have been about this time that our maid, who was pretty and twice as old as I was, caught me in the hallway, pulled me into the pantry and began to teach me a few essentials about life using practical examples. It was the last and most beautiful game I learned in those childhood days. We never played the game to its finish, though.

After these events, I did not see why I had to spend my evenings eavesdropping at the doors of clubs. I already knew a few of the musicians who came and went. They made fun of me in a nice way. Now it was time to show them! I started visiting my relatives in the Barnyard Quarter more often and collected a fair amount of change. I grabbed a couple of friends from my clique and said: "Come on, today we're going to the *Dorette*!" It was one of my favorite clubs on Kantstrasse. I could not know I would be playing there myself in the not too distant future.

On that day I actually made it inside accompanied by my older friends; we sat at a table directly facing the dance floor. As long as I sat in my chair, it was hard to tell my age. For the first time I soaked up the atmosphere of Berlin's nightlife and enjoyed the vibrating air, the smoke, the smell of dancing people. It didn't take long for a girl to ask me for a dance. Two heads taller than me, she noticed my hesitation from above and had a splendid idea: the dance floor was a little bit elevated, so she decided: "I'll dance below and you dance above!" Wonderful. The world had once again expanded significantly. The music worked like a drug that inebriated me – and nothing has changed about that since then.

In addition to my enthusiasm for music, I had a second passion that began to be more useful. I was always up for a fight, even when I was younger, when we lived in Rudow. When my mom picked me up from school in those days she would ask: "Where's Schumann?" The custodian blinked at her in astonishment: "Who? Oh, you mean Schmeling (famous boxer Max Schmeling)! Well, he's in a fight over there!"

I had joined a Jewish sports club, *Bar Kochba*, a club in the national association "Makkabi in Germany" and had tried out a few types of sports. I was not a bad swimmer and had won a few competitions; I was quite good at the short distance races but did not have much endurance. I asked the boxing trainer if I could try out the punching bag. I threw some punches at it that almost tore it up, and my punches were technically not that bad. My trainer was so surprised he had to laugh and thought I was a natural. I trained faithfully after that and managed to win a number of boxing matches. The scars of my split eyebrows still tell one or the other story.

Unfortunately those boxing matches only happened inside my club – a Jewish boxer could not smash in the nose of an "Aryan" boxer in those days. But outside on the streets, there were plenty of opportunities to apply the lessons learned in a practical manner. When a group of Hitler Youth strode past and thought they could rough me up, I faced them as long as their number was manageable, put my back up against a wall and gave them a beating that left them thinking. After my sports club was forced to close the following year, I smashed in the nose of anybody who called me a "Jew", just to stay in shape.

The year of 1938 saw decisive changes, even though I did not acknowledge the seriousness of the situation or did not want to, having such a sunny, young disposition. I registered that my country had annexed Austria to form a *Grossdeutsches Reich* (Greater German Empire), but I didn't care. In summer the Munich and the Nuremberg synagogues were destroyed, but it was beyond the limited horizon of my fourteen years. Like any teenager, I thought current events and daily news did not have anything to do with my life. I adapted to the circumstances, considered myself to be a Berliner and believed that the "disharmony" us Jews had to live with would soon eventually be resolved – and, above all, that the day would come when I could, if I wanted to, become a member of the Hitler Youth, even if I was not "eligible" anymore. I was not concerned about political developments.

It was, however, a sensation that a cousin of mine who was drafted gave me his Wandergitarre before he left. I finally had my own guitar and could play my favorite kind of music on it more or less clumsily.

I was forced to leave my school in Halensee and go to a school of the Jewish Reform Community that was on Joachimsthaler Strasse. I did not learn much there since the teachers were constantly leaving and being replaced; one after the other left Germany. One teacher however did make a difference in my life: Dr. Ballin. He taught German and would occasionally bring along his guitar to lighten the mood in the classroom. All of the kids liked him a lot. When I asked him if he could teach me something on his guitar, he said yes. He showed me the first chords and some subtle rhythms. I heard Django Reinhardt recordings for the first time, which left a big impression on me.

I practiced every day like I was possessed, chords and scales, up and down, down and up. I had a definite rhythm going from the first day – one I was not aware of. Later somebody told me it was a mix between the melancholy of Django Reinhardt and the rhythmic comping of Freddie Green, Count Basie's faithful sideman. I didn't know much about that back then. I just played from my guts, from the very beginning.

Apart from jazz, I had the Jewish music of my childhood in my ears. Something connected both of them. Jewish music swings on its own. A lot of great American swing composers grew up in Jewish immigrant families from Rumania, Hungary and Russia. George Gershwin, Irving Berlin, and Benny Goodman – if they weren't black they were Jewish, and they brought their tradition along with them into this music.

Strictly speaking, jazz developed from the collision of African and European, mostly Jewish musical culture in America. The mix was not without its problems. What I could not have known in 1938 was that there were mixed bands in America since about a year after Benny Goodman had hired the piano player Teddy Wilson and that the walls that separated the races finally collapsed at the Carnegie Hall concert in January 1938 – the exact opposite of what was happening in the Grossdeutsche Reich.

In October of that year, while cruising through the Charlottenburg bars, I noticed for the first time handbills that said *Swing tanzen verboten* – Swing dancing prohibited, which certainly did not bother me much at the time. Something else had happened that opened my eyes in a major way. I earned some pocket money working a part-time job after school for a plumber named Herr Aron. He lived at the Rosenthaler Platz. Since non-Aryan artisans were not allowed to work in that district, a few Jewish plumbers, electricians and carpenters were able to continue their businesses with special permit. A convenient side effect of all this was that my mom, who was horrified by my desire to become a musician, calmed down. She hoped that I would still get a firm footing in life by learning a trade. She had already forbidden any further guitar lessons, so I paid for my last lessons with Dr. Ballin with money my dad had surreptitiously slipped into my pocket for that purpose. Until one day when even Dr. Ballin left the country.

On the evening of November 9, 1938, I stepped out of Mr. Aron's workshop into the street. I do not know why, but there was a strange unsettling silence in the air. A fire alarm went off in the distance; a short time later another one went off, then another, until what became known as the *Reichskristallnacht* broke out around me – the Night of Broken Glass. Trucks drove through the streets, thugs armed with clubs jumped from them and smashed shop windows and kicked in doors, stormed houses and drove the people living in them out into the streets. I saw, not understanding what I was watching, how people were pushed out of windows or jumped from them because they were terrified. The merchandise in the shop windows was scattered on the sidewalks, everything inside was smashed up. The air was filled with the screams of the murderers and their victims, the noise of alarm bells and klaxons and then with acrid smoke.

I ran as fast as I could to Uncle Arthur's hair salon on Alte Schönhauser Strasse. Nobody had touched his shop yet. I told him what was happening. I do not know how, but he managed to pull all the levers he could, saved his shop and protected the lives and businesses of our relatives from destruction. Maybe his

Broken shop window of a Jewish-owned business destroyed during the Kristallnacht pogrom.
Berlin, November 10, 1938
UNITED STATES HOLOCAUST MEMORIAL MUSEUM,
COURTESY OF NATIONAL ARCHIVES AND RECORDS ADMINISTRATION, COLLEGE PARK

friendship with the sons of the former police chief Hellmann had proven to be useful.

After this night and the ongoing pogroms that continued on the following two days, Uncle Arthur decided to leave the country. His contacts in the better circles of society were helpful. He got the necessary papers through a friend who worked in the Bolivian consulate, destination La Paz, and proceeded to pack his enormous shipping trunk with his best pieces of clothing. I can still see it: a white smoking jacket hung in front – a sight that made me want to be like him more than ever. That this would come partially true was something I could only hope for in those days. The first sign that this would happen was the fact that he left me his drum set – a cymbal, a hi-hat and a drum with a red light under the drumhead.

A few days later a decree took effect that excluded Jewish children from all public schools. I spent a few days with the plumber, Mr. Aron, until all Jewish businesses had been expropriated by December – including my mom's hair salon. We had to give up our apartment on Kronprinzendamm with the view over the railroad tracks, where hundreds of freight cars passed through every day, because three Jews were no longer permitted to live in five-bedroom apartments. We moved into a small courtyard apartment on Kurfürstenstrasse.

The *Wehrmacht Nachrichtentruppe* (Army Signal Corps) and Waffen SS instruct Hitler Youth
Location unknown, August 1938
COURTESY: BUNDESARCHIV

As tough as our living conditions had become, my parents could not decide whether to leave Germany or not. For one thing, we did not have enough money – although we could have borrowed from family members – for another, we could not believe all this was happening. Due to the fact that my mother's side of the family kept its distance from the Orthodox Jews and that my father's side felt a strong bond to its native country, the fatal assumption settled in our minds that everything would work out somehow – that we would be able to make some arrangement with the new regime, which could not continue this way forever. Vigorous arguments about this issue boiled over shortly before Arthur's departure. He was the most adventurous member of the family, and perhaps his worldly experience provided him with the most realistic perspective among us. But he could not convince us to do likewise.

I thought our situation was relatively harmless. I was too young and too naive to seriously consider leaving Germany or to think about a personal engagement in these matters. I wanted to struggle through daily affairs, fit in. I would "escape" from reality practicing my guitar and my drums every day for several hours, trying out different styles and tricks. Music was my life, and I didn't care about anything else. The guys in my clique did not know I was a Jew, and I did not tell them. I had no reason to do so. Ideas about liberty and the light-hearted playfulness of

Handmade Star of David worn by French "Zazous" (Swings) to demonstrate against Nazi occupation and imposition of German laws

The student who displayed this badge, Maurice Lombart, was arrested in Paris, 1942.

the Berlin swing scene did collide with the compulsory youth service in March of 1939, but unlike the scene in Hamburg, the Berlin swing scene did not consider joining the resistance.

Most swing fans felt they were "real" Germans; members of the Youth League (10-14) and the Hitler Youth (14-18), born and raised under the sign of the National Socialist rule, were embedded in it and part of it. The "resistance" of swing found its expression in teenage rebellion, if at all: we insisted on our predilections and entertainment and felt deep disdain for military hierarchies, for marching in lockstep and the music that went along with that. We did not have foresight. So most of us did not react to the signs of the times.

When Teddy Stauffer left Germany for good in 1939 – he later wrote in his biography that Billy Toffel and himself had decided to emigrate during Kristallnacht, on November 9, 1938 – and the propaganda kept calling swing a plague that had to be fought with every means available, the nightlife of Berlin did not miss a beat, nor did we. Every time things got more dramatic, such as the general call to serve in national works programs, the invasion of Czechoslovakia, the rationing of essential goods, people got more excited about swing and jazz, as a compensation, a way to avoid reality.

Later on, I read about unambiguous solidarity declarations made by the

"Zazous", the Parisian swing scene, for Jews in occupied France: a group of non-Jewish young people ran through the streets waving a banner bearing the Star of David with the word "Swing" stitched across it. There was not any comparable will of resistance in the circles in which I moved.

While German soldiers were crossing the border with Poland on September 1, 1939, the beginning of World War II, my group sat on the banks of the Lietzensee (Lake Lietzen) listening to my attempts to play the guitar before we started out on our trip visiting the bars on Kurfürstendamm. At the *Melody Bar,* I heard a violinist named Helmut Zacharias. He was nineteen years old, had on a pair of shortened shepherd's check pants and could play swing like he had invented it. He fascinated me with his extraordinary gift for combining his academic skill with an incredible ability to improvise. He was a kind of child prodigy: he had begun to play the violin when he was four years old, at the age of six he was already conducting his father's orchestra at the cabaret *Faun* and now he had just returned from a European tour with the Berlin Chamber Orchestra organized by the Odeon Record Company. In short, he had great success as a solo jazz player. His playing was reminiscent of the motto placed over the enchanted world of the *Delphi*: "Sweet Forgetfulness".

The regime urgently tried to satisfy the public's need for entertainment. This was evident from the fact that they had lifted the ban they had placed on all public dance clubs only three weeks earlier. The fake "normality" was indispensable. The decree to implement the "Extraordinary Decree Governing Radio Broadcasting" which "prohibited the intentional listening to foreign radio programming" was of little interest to us, just as the general prohibition of English music following the declaration of war on Great Britain.

We became familiar faces in the joints we visited night after night; we knew the staff and the owners. In December of that year, the owner of the *Hasenschaukel* on Pestalozzistrasse asked me to accompany his piano player on New Year's Eve playing drums. My first job as a musician! To my parent's great consternation I strapped Uncle Arthur's drum kit onto my back and trudged through the darkened, snow-filled streets to my "workplace". I was paid five marks, which I immediately invested in the remainder of the evening – because my premiere that evening was unforgettable in more than just the musical sense.

During the first set we had exchanged suggestive looks. She was extremely attractive, and I was unusually riled up, so I pulled her out into the night during the first break. The moon was shining down onto the white snow of the Lietzenseepark where over a foot and a half of fresh snow covered the benches.

Finally we found each other, balancing on two to three legs, exploring what the maid in our apartment on Kronprinzendamm had concealed from me.

The employment office had assigned me to a master plumber in Charlottenburg as required by the national works program. The situation left me feeling very unsatisfied, having to haul cast iron radiators up to the fourth floor of a new building for fifty cents an hour, or, later on, fitting new water pipes in a bombed-out building while my friends could devote themselves to music or their studies.

But at least with my modest income and a couple of fees, I was able to buy my first good guitar from a member of a gypsy band, with a bridge and f-holes. It was self-made, and since there were no amplifiers around, it was so big that my pals would say: "Here comes Coco with his grandma!"

Starting in spring of 1940, I took advantage of every opportunity to play with a variety of bands, sitting in for a couple of tunes. The leader of a gypsy band that was playing the *Café am Steinplatz* asked me if I would like to play guitar with his band. I did not know too many chords, but I knew how to swing and word had gotten around.

I got my first regular engagement at the *Allotria-Bar* on Leibnizstrasse with another gypsy band. Tassilo played bass fiddle, but I have forgotten the other names except for one: Botho Lucas, who later founded the famous choir of the same name. He was an excellent musician even back then, an accordion virtuoso who played Heinz Monsonius and Albert Vossen's difficult pieces. I admired him for his skill and for the fact that he had actually studied his instrument, unlike myself.

But life being what it is, it was him of all people who showed me how I could take matters into my own hands. The first day I tried to play original Hungarian gypsy music, I felt somewhat lost. As soon as Lucas noticed, he moved over next to me with his squeezebox and whispered the chords and harmonies as we played. After a few numbers I was more confident, I learned them and added my own style. I was convinced I could learn purely by listening and playing in front of an audience. It was fantastic to feel that day by day I was learning my profession, one small step at a time. Every night I felt reborn. The dance clubs and bars were raking it in; the gap between day and the nightlife was so large that, looking back, I could not understand how the two could ever form a whole. The *Rosita Bar* was a hangout where I could even play with George Trapp's UFA dance band; my friend Rudy Ernst on drums, myself on guitar. The drummer Willy Kettel stood in front of me, laughed and shouted to his colleagues: "Listen to that kid – not bad!" Experiences like this motivated me tremendously.

We also liked to hang out at the legendary *Groschenkeller* at 126 Kantstrasse, opened by the writer Franz Jung. Every night there was a strange mix of people: teenage movie star Hannelore Schroth, the daughter of actress Käte Haack; singer Evelyn Künnecke; Helmut Zacharias and his girlfriend and later wife, Hella, a dancer; a soprano from the national opera; guys who drove beer trucks and construction workers – the swing scene produced an inexhaustible gallery of characters. A young man by the name of Bully Buhlan sat at the piano and sang. We got to know each other one evening and before long we were jamming together. The success we had was incomprehensible, considering that I did not really have that much skill, and more so as stars like guitarist Serge Matul performed here, someone I really admired. The *Groschenkeller* was my world. I had the feeling that I just had to play what was coming out from inside of me. Maybe it was the slight variations in my rhythm, hidden eccentricities. Whatever it was, it worked.

From that evening on, I appeared regularly on stage as a guest player, even if my pay consisted of free drinks only – a stew we called "tangled wire" – and a friendly glance from one of the bearded bartender's two daughters. One after another, exciting evenings came and went, every evening bringing new celebrities. Norbert Schultze, for example, who sat down right in front of the stage and was thrilled by the music. After all, he didn't know about my heritage, a heritage that would not have pleased the composer of *Bombem auf England* and *Lili Marleen*.

One evening a man with a very distinguished appearance sat down in front of me, looked intently at what I was doing and spoke to me during the break. "Very nice what you are playing. Would you like to study with me? I can show you a few things." I was somewhat surprised. "Who are you?" "Oh, sorry. Hans Korseck is the name." Hans Korseck – bull's-eye! An encounter with God Almighty! I only knew about him from his recordings: the best guitar player that I had ever heard. He had jammed with Benny Goodman. Now he was asking me, a *steppke* (little boy) if . . . I almost fell off my chair.

I regularly went to his place at Fasanenstrasse 13 to take lessons. First he taught me the fundamentals for the many chords I didn't know, as well as his incomparable American rhythm technique, which nicely complemented what I was doing by instinct. Just like Helmut Zacharias and Bully Buhlan, he did not ask any questions. They sensed that there was something hidden, but as they say in Berlin, "You really don't have to pay attention to ignore that . . ."

Bully Buhlan hired me for his gig at the *Rosendiele*, one of the legendary jazz clubs in Berlin – the band leader Kurt Widmann started his career there – and at *Arnd's Bier Bar* at Olivaer Platz. All of this was very uplifting for me. On the one hand, my new status as a musician attracted the attention of the ladies; on the other hand, I could take my day job laying pipes less seriously thanks to the extra cash from my evening work. I acquired the stamina necessary for the long days and nights thanks to the bonuses of the pub owners and through a friend from the *Groschenkeller*, Coco Petrovich, a very elegant man.

As the son of a diplomat, he had a good number of food ration coupons in his pocket. The days I called in sick instead of going to work at the plumber's began to add up. I would rather go cruising around town, go to the Kurfürstendamm with him and stop by at *Mampe's* where we would eat our fill. We smoked like chimneys and tried to keep up with the fashion of the day: short hair like the movie star Jopie Heesters or long hair combed back to the collar, a long, double-breasted jacket, razor sharp creases (not a given in those days) and the mandatory hat. Everything had to click together in our tiny, unreal counter-world, a world surrounded by war.

Nothing could have stopped me from living my life with music or from living in a constant state of near euphoria. It was just the reverse: the same mindlessness that led me to believe I could wear the uniform of the Youth League at school caused me to believe the Nazis would let me become a member of the Reichsmusikkammer so that I could pursue my dream career, officially and state-approved . . . Even if they were trying to stamp out swing and jazz, they would never be able to eradicate it completely.

The police were patrolling the bars and clubs in Berlin in cooperation with the Gestapo. While we were swinging, there would always be somebody at the door keeping an eye open for anyone who looked suspicious. If a police patrol came by, somebody whistled and the band would change the beat on the proverbial dime. If we were playing *Tiger Rag* we changed to *Rosamunde* before the cops came through the door. After a stern glance at the customers, a smile from the pub owner and a short wait for the all clear sign once the snitch had disappeared around the next corner, we were playing *You Can't Stop Me from Dreaming* once again.

A variation of this camouflage was to "Germanize" the English lyrics. We were able to buy any number of English and American records under the table, and soldiers returning from neighboring countries brought more records to Berlin. It was a lot easier to modify the original tune, play it ourselves and disguise it with harmless German titles like *Sie will nicht Blumen und nicht Schokolade* (She Doesn't Want Flowers or Chocolate) instead of the original Andrew Sister's hit *Joseph! Joseph!* (a song that in certain circles served to ridicule Joseph Goebbels,

Coco Schumann (guitar), Rudi Ernst (clarinet), Ilja Glusgal (percussion) and companion at the Wannseebad, 1940

Ilja Glusgal, Rudi Ernst and Coco Schumann

Coco Schumann (guitar) and Rudi Ernst (clarinet) at the *Groschenkeller*, Berlin, 1940

the Propaganda Minister of the Nazi regime). Louis Armstrong's hit, *I Can't Give You Anything but Love, Baby* became *Ist dein kleines Herz noch für mich frei, Baby?* (Is Your Little Heart Still Free For Me, Baby?). Fred Oldörp conjured up his hit *Hallo kleines Fräulein* (Hello, Little Miss) from *Sweet Georgia Brown* and Ella Fitzgerald's hit song, *A Tisket, a Tasket*, became the incredibly popular children's song, *Laterne, Laterne* (Lantern, Lantern).

Even numerous card-carrying national socialists did not give up their love of swing music. The officials in charge did not seem to see through our game of "Germanizing" the titles of jazz songs. We often had the feeling that we could get away with this forever. We did not notice that they actually saw through our sham a lot of the time, but they let us get away with it because they liked what we were doing, or for practical reasons.

On this stage of danger and passion, politics and music, Walter Mittler was a particularly colorful character. Mittler was an official at the Ministry of Propaganda and particularly inscrutable. He produced programs for the Overseas German Broadcasting Network to motivate German soldiers and to mislead the enemy. He was looking for the "scene" again in order to show the British how well we were doing and how much fun we were having in Germany.

When he drove up to the *Groschenkeller* we knew right away that the jig was up. Mittler was as easy to recognize as a dog painted blue, driving an open MG that had flower boxes strapped to it, an open umbrella in hand. All the girls he knew – and he acted like there were a lot of them – had left lipstick kisses on the windows and the hood of the car. It was impressive the way he could dance between the lines while playing the fool.

When he came down to the basement, Ilja Glusgal, Helmut Zacharias and I were playing. Mittler shouted, "Let 'er rip!", setting up a microphone and hooking it up to a radio truck parked outside where the program was recorded on wax discs common to those days. At first we didn't know what to do; we thought he would take us right to jail, but we let it rip. What else *could* we do? Ilja played a hot rendition of a Cab Calloway number; he could sing scat improvisations that were just wonderful – that is, he could sing a series of unintelligible lyrics really fast. The audience went mad. Mittler was happy. We had him so worked up that he even sang a few songs himself at the end of the set and closed by saying, "If my propaganda minister hears this I get a one-way ticket to a concentration camp." He didn't know how right he was. He only later realized that his microphone was live and his comments had been cut into a wax disc! He must have gotten along fine with his crew because his comment about the propaganda minister was erased.

The "Police Edict Concerning the Protection of Minors" that prohibited everyone under the age of twenty-one from being anywhere but home after six o'clock was not meant to protect us from the night so much as to protect the night from us. I really do not need to mention here that we ignored it. But this mix of naiveté and brazenness was becoming more dicey. I no longer would have stood a chance in hell of simply being put into a *Jugendschutzlager* (juvenile detention facility). They would not have been satisfied with just shaving the head of a swing fan, the usual punishment for long hair. But so what? The first bombs were falling around us now, and they were reason enough to doubt one's survival into tomorrow. We wanted our fun today.

Nazi Germany occupied France and completed Auschwitz at about the same time we were frolicking on the beaches of the Wannsee, forbidden for Jews for a long time now, or on the C-Deck of the beach pool. It was noted for its cosmopolitan air and was a hangout for everybody who was *mampe* – half and half – like the famous liqueur of Frau Mampe, that is, half-Jewish – a typical Berlin pun on the Hebrew word for a half breed, *mamser*. The C-Deck was one of these zones where you could get around almost all the prohibitions and regulations.

We could only laugh at the notorious Zwickel Edict, which, among other things, determined the amount of skin we were allowed to expose, the girls fortunately as well; we were pretty liberal. There we sat, three *mampes*, Rudi

Ernst with the clarinet, Ilja Glusgal the flamboyant vocalist and myself with my "grandmother" guitar, surrounded by lovely womanliness, swinging *Flat foot floogee with the floy-floy* and feeling that all would be well.

Alles wird gut ("all will be well") meant both hope and escape. This state of mind was also quite well known outside of Germany and was catered to accordingly. The English BBC was broadcasting a propaganda program dubbed *Germany Calling, Germany Calling . . .* which by now could cost you your life if you listened to it. The first four notes of Beethoven's Fifth Symphony were used as the program's theme song. If you wanted to listen to the program and had found a safe place you turned the knob on the radio until hearing the melody.

We decided to use those four notes as our signature: "All will be well" was considered to be a synonym. When two swing fans met and were not sure who they were talking to, one of them would grab a button on his jacket and turn it slowly, like a radio dial. The other one would answer *"Alles wird gut"*. It took a while for the fake guys to figure it out.

It was a wonderful impertinence for a famous big band like Ernst van't Hoff's to choose these notes as its signature theme. The band was fantastic and highly regarded by us. They played with a genuine American sound. One day Ernst van't Hoff asked me if I could fill in for his guitar player who was in Holland for a few days. I had taken offers like this in stride before, but now I was so excited I couldn't sleep the night before. It was not entirely *Alles wird gut,* but at least that one evening was spectacular.

We did not even hear much about the beginning of the *Endlösung der Judenfrage*, the Final Solution of the Jewish Question, in August of 1941. Maybe the headwind was blowing a little stronger. We did not want to believe the rumors circulating at the time; they were too horrific, and life was too exciting. I acknowledged the torture and murder of Aunt Hanni's Polish husband at the Sachsenhausen concentration camp, but I saw it as a tragic and horrible isolated case. I did not want to think about how many tragic "isolated cases" had occurred already and how many millions more would follow.

In September it became mandatory to wear the Star of David. Contrary to the "half-Jews 1st class", this included myself as I had become a full member of the Jewish community when celebrating my bar mitzvah. I didn't care much: instead of wearing it on my lapel I preferred to keep it in my pocket. My blue eyes and Berlin wise-guy talk did not fit the stereotype of the typical Jew.

If I ran into a checkpoint, I headed straight for it and, using my harshest Berlin accent, said: "Say, how do I get to such-and-such street from here?" before they could ask me for my papers. After they gave me the directions in the most polite and friendly manner, I swerved past these gentlemen as elegantly as I could and got myself to a safe place.

There was no "Jewish Question" among swing musicians. Nobody talked about it even though some of us thought about it or sensed something. Jews were playing in famous bands, whether with real or with fake papers. If we had talked about it, we would have put ourselves in danger because we never knew who was standing next to us. The safest thing for all of us was to keep silent and to turn the chaotic circumstances of the times to our own personal advantage. The law enforcement agencies were no longer able to run orderly checkpoints or maintain real control. A lot of people in Berlin had died, and in just a few months the population of the city had swollen by at least a hundred thousand refugees from the surrounding regions, who also enriched the music scene and nightlife.

When I look back at those times, I think I was incredibly lucky to muddle through for that long without having to go into hiding. The deportations had started long ago. By then, since 1933, almost ten million people had been sent to concentration camps, however, we knew next to nothing as to the scale of these events. My strategy was to hide in plain sight. I did numerous recordings and performances with Werner Neumann's radio orchestra for the Berlin Broadcasting Network. My name was mentioned, but I could always avoid having to sign anything official.

The only major problem was how to get into the lion's den. Helmut Zacharias and Werner Müller, who would later conduct the RIAS (*Radio Im Amerikanischen Sector*) dance orchestra after the war, wanted to rehearse for a recording – at the Lankwitz barracks, where they were both stationed as radio operators at the time. The "watchdogs", members of the *Leibstandarte* Adolf Hitler, were standing at the gate, shiny badges and chains on their black uniforms. Helmut and Werner were supposed to pick me up at the entrance. Flanked by two celebrities, I waved at these beasts as I passed them. Nobody ever asked for my ID, not even once.

I played the *Rosita Bar* during the early part of 1942 with Tullio Mobiglia's sextet. He was an Italian, "the most beautiful saxophone player in the world" as he liked to call himself. He was not entirely wrong about that; he had an audacious, extremely elegant air about him. He had been a student of the best saxophone player in the world, Coleman Hawkins, and the way he led his sextet was unorthodox. We had to play all the American swing standards without a score, which really gave us a powerful incentive to improvise.

The audience considered Tullio's sextet to be the best small jazz formation

Tullio Mobiglia, "The Most Beautiful
Saxophone Player in the World",
artist photo signed for Coco
Schumann, 1942

Rosita-Bar advertisement

then playing in the Reich. I felt safe among the Italians; nobody asked any questions when they said I was from Milan. We got along great, had lots of gigs and had to take care of a lot of groupies. That was about it.

Tullio broke the hearts of a considerable number of women, and I found a way to be part of that. After all, I was seventeen and wanted to enjoy life for as long as possible. On stage we had ample opportunity to talk about the girls in the audience without the uninitiated ones noticing. We had an advantage over bands that played from sheets of music as we could watch their reaction the whole time.

We used the classical language of musicians to communicate on stage, Pig Latin. We would take the last syllable of a word and move it to the front so that a sentence might come out like this: *eckchay touay ethay ondeblay at abletay reethay,* (check out the blonde at table three), for example. Or we communicated with our instruments to tell each other which girl we would pursue after the set. It was my job to court the ladies during the break and ask, "Are you doing anything after the show? Mr. Mobiglia would love to meet you." Most of them blushed when I propositioned them and agreed with a nod.

I got the name "Coco" around this time, the name that would remain with me all my life. A French girlfriend who – what else is new – could not pronounce the letter "H" kept calling me "einz", which got on my nerves after a while. "Okay," she said, "then I'll call you *Chéri Coco*". Well, thanks a lot! At first I was not exactly thrilled by this moniker, but when I asked some multilingual friends about it I learned that my new name could have several meanings – from "coconut" to "rascal" to "darling" to "belly". She thought that what my girlfriend meant, though, was "little chicken", if not "rooster", and that she meant it in a friendly way. Then I was announced this way, and I noticed it did not sound bad at all – without the "*Chéri*". When the first recording came out with this name, the case was settled for good.

By the standards of the time, I was earning some serious coin playing for Mobiglia. Working as a plumber's apprentice, which I still did "on the side", I earned fifty cents an hour; with a forty-eight-hour week I was taking home 100 reichsmark a month, less taxes and the "Jew tax". My foreman smoked Juno, three for a penny, while I crammed my pockets full of the Nil cigars I had gotten on the black market and wore a brilliant-cut ring on my finger. I earned 800 marks a month playing at the *Rosita Bar,* and for each day I was on the set of a feature film, I got another 100.

As members of the Mobiglia Orchestra, we were hired for various movies by Tobis to be elegant extras in movies like *Die Philharmoniker,* directed by Paul

Verhoeven and starring Kirsten Heiberg and Will Quadflieg. The latter was playing a young violinist in a hot dance band, who, as the promotion department explained, "has to rid himself of his impetuosity before he can take up his calling". As far as I know the takes showing us were cut out later. I had a good understanding with a doctor friend who would write me up sick if I needed.

There was a little problem posed by the cash payments made at the end of a day's shoot. I could not use my name since I was registered as a Jew with the tax authorities and was not a member of the Reichsmusikkammer, so if I gave my name the jig would be up. Fortunately, I found another Heinz Schumann in the phone book, a chauffeur, whose identity I assumed. I don't suppose he suffered much because of my deception during the growing confusion the war brought with it.

I was able to make a comfortable living and help my family, too. My parents had difficulties under these circumstances because people who lived in mixed marriages were given less and less food stamps. I could get some things for them, but without the help of their neighbors and friends they would have had real problems, particularly when my brother Jürgen was born in 1942.

One of my mother's former customers, the wife of a butcher, discovered the reason why my mother had to close up her hair salon. She came to our home to have her hair done, bartering meat from their butcher shop since my mom and dad could not get food ration cards for meat. This woman and others like her are the reason that to this very day I cannot blame "the Germans" collectively for what happened.

On February 18, 1943, the minister of propaganda Joseph Goebbels proclaimed "total war" at the Sportpalast in Berlin; the answer by the Allies did not take long. They began to bomb larger areas of Berlin. We saw apartment buildings break apart from the force of the explosions or shoot up in flames like torches made of straw. If it rained, the billowing smoke and ash condensed to the ground where it formed a sludge that stuck to the soles of our shoes. It was hard to walk, exhausting and bleak. But we kept on playing, whether in bars or air raid shelters, even if our "procession through town" encountered a gray stream of hunched over figures: mostly bombed-out victims of air raids who, carrying everything they had left with them, seemed to appear out of nowhere and disappear back into nothingness. We kept on playing even when day was no longer distinguishable from night, when after an air raid darkness would fall over the streets like it was evening, when parts of Berlin would become as black as night even though it was the middle of the day – we kept on playing. Even if many of our friends lost their

Nazi rally filmed at the Berlin *Sportpalast*, February 18, 1943
Propaganda Minister Joseph Goebbels urged Germans toward further sacrifice
in "a war more total and radical than anything that we can even yet imagine".
The banner reads "Totaler Krieg – Kürzester Krieg" ("Total War – Shortest War").

lives or were interned or fell on the battlefield – friends like Hans Korseck, who was just thirty-one – we kept on playing. It was as if we were possessed. The only thing that counted was today; tomorrow was uncertain.

I drifted carelessly and recklessly through an increasingly apocalyptic environment towards an unknown, dark abyss. My naiveté led me to drink my cup of good fortune down to the last drop. The SS conducted a raid on the *Rosita Bar*. They were looking for deserters, people on the lam and minors, and searched the bar thoroughly. But one of the SS men stood in front of the bandstand, clapping his hands with much enthusiasm. He brought out the devil in me. I stood up and said, "Actually, you have to arrest me!" He looked bewildered. "Why?" "Well, I'm a Jew, I play swing and I'm a minor." He laughed out loud and could not stop laughing at this stupendous joke. The entire bar roared with him.

My parents, who had given up trying to guide me toward a more cautious way of life, had tried to protect me the previous year by having Father Pohl, a Lutheran priest, baptize me, but by then officials had already stopped accepting such obvious maneuvers.

Then the curtain fell. In March 1943 a criminal investigation unit ordered me to report to them. I was accused of failing to wear my Star of David, performing forbidden music and seducing Aryan women. Much later I learned the real reason for my arrest. The scene I moved in was largely apolitical. If anyone were active in a conspiratorial manner, they would keep everyone, even their best friend, in the dark. Anybody who did anything, and anybody who knew about it, was not only in great danger but a great danger to others as well.

The year before, I had visited a cousin of mine, Heinz Rothholz, and a couple of his friends at their hangout, a basement. I played guitar, we were in a good mood and shot off our mouths. What I did not know was that the moderately "critical" conversation was already a cover. Some of them were members of an illegal group with Herbert Baum and had been politically active for years. My cousin was a member of that group. Shortly after a propaganda show called *Das Sowjetparadies* (The Soviet Paradise) had opened in the spring of 1942 at the summer garden on Museum Island, part of the exhibition went up in flames. Two days later – as we later learned – Heinz and other members of our happy round were guillotined. An informer for the Gestapo had slipped into our group and listened to me playing the guitar. I would have never suspected anything like that. My simplemindedness was apparently so obvious I was only placed under surveillance.

Obediently, I marched off to the gathering place on Grosse Hamburger Strasse, into the formerly Jewish Hospital, convinced I could talk my way out. They kept me there and told me I had been assigned to the next train to Auschwitz.

I did not know what was happening in the East but it must have been horrible, I was certain about that. However, I had also heard of camps that were more or less bearable. My grandmother and grandfather had been deported to Theresienstadt a few weeks earlier and had sent back a – preprinted – postcard. My dad ran over to Grosse Hamburger Strasse as soon as he heard what had happened and tried to help me. He presented himself to Walter Dobberke, showed his Aryan ID card and pleaded with him – for my life. He had fought in the war, had been poisoned with mustard gas for his fatherland and had done everything he could to imprint his German patriotism on me. Could he at least transfer me to be with my grandparents in Theresienstadt . . .

He was able to soften the stone-cold Dobberke. I was already standing in line for the Auschwitz transport and had worked my way to the front of the line to the registrar's table when I heard a voice roaring through the room: "Schumann, step back!" My guardian angel had worked overtime.

Avant de Mourir

THERESIENSTADT was a not-particularly-large, fortress-like settlement, a former Austro-Hungarian garrison called Terezín that was built on the border with Czechoslovakia in what was then the Protectorate of Bohemia and Moravia. There were forty large blocks of multi-story barracks, once named after German cities but now identified only by letters and numbers. They surrounded a central marketplace and lay symmetrically along a grid pattern of streets that measured approximately one thousand by five hundred yards. They bore common street names: Wallstrasse, Lange Strasse, Badhausgasse, Seestrassse and Bahnhofstrasse.

This is how we arrived: approximately forty or fifty inmates were crammed inside each boxcar and each inmate carried about thirty pounds of luggage. When I climbed down onto the platform I was surprised, almost relieved, to see an actual small town in front of me. Perhaps this kind of relief can only be explained by the fact that I had avoided the transport to Auschwitz. Whatever awaited me now, it couldn't be that bad.

After the guards, the Czech police and the SS had finished confiscating our luggage and all of our valuables inside a building they called "the sluice" and had completed our obligatory delousing in a "bathhouse", I went straightaway to look for my grandparents. I knew from the times I had roamed the Barnyard Quarter where I needed to look. It was exactly the way I imagined. I found him in the courtyard of a nearby block of barracks, shaving. He still wore his beard proudly, like the Kaiser. Men whose ribs were sticking out stood in line in front of him.

To those old soldiers, to front line troops, to men who had been awarded the Iron Cross, who were proud and good enough to have fought for their country, ready to give their lives, but who were not permitted to live in it now, the camp was grotesque. Their universal incomprehension stood beyond the naked threat to their lives: humiliated, loathed, imprisoned and maybe soon murdered by the same hand all of them had once believed in. An entirely different situation than the one I was facing with my nineteen carefree years. Under these circumstances the greeting of my grandparents turned out to be strange. Who could say "It's nice to see you here ..."? Of course we were happy to see each other, but we were not happy about the circumstances of our reunion – because this reunion was more of a final farewell than a reencounter.

Later I explored the camp and could hardly believe my eyes. A strange illusion appeared. Mostly privileged Jews – or whatever you might call them under the circumstances – came to Theresienstadt: artists and intellectuals, people from prestigious professions, well-known people from the Jewish community, athletes, scholars, children – and those *mampes* from Germany and annexed countries like Holland, Austria, Hungary, France, Czechoslovakia and Denmark – a crowd of "extras" of every sort who were needed on the set to play their part in this bizarre theater of our life in the camp, pretending all was well. Theresienstadt was one giant illusion of internal and external propaganda, a place to hide from the attentive gazes of other countries and the International Red Cross. Behind the scenes, there was only one director – death.

In some of the larger cities, agencies would sell a "claim" to a residence in this beautiful senior "resort" to elderly Jews and to well-to-do Jews who were living alone, for a lot of money. What cynicism! While Theresienstadt was a place people like me could endure, it meant something altogether different for the elderly who had invested their life's savings in the hope of a quiet, peaceful retirement among their peers, only to end up living in stinking dumps made from stinking casemates. It was a terrible insult and humiliation. The naked perfidy, organized with incomprehensible thoroughness, kept most of us and the other inmates from even thinking about not playing the game.

I ran down the main street and could not comprehend what I was seeing. Even at first glance the conditions in the camp were intolerable due to the fact that it had been built to house seven thousand Czechs and now held about fifty nine thousand prisoners. Nevertheless, the scenery was confusing. I discovered small parks and – even though it was locked up – a church.

When I turned around, already slightly irritated, looking over the market place, I could not believe my eyes. There was a coffee house in the middle of the camp, and I could hear familiar music coming from inside, music that was my music. Nothing could hold me back now! I ran over and discovered I could not get inside without a ticket, so I ran around the outside of the coffee house. I

Aerial view of the ghetto from the Nazi propaganda film _Theresienstadt – A Documentary Film about the Jewish Resettlement_
COLLECTION OF YAD VASHEM

Ghetto money in Theresienstadt
COLLECTION OF YAD VASHEM

didn't see any guards. When I was finally able to get in through the back door, the music stopped. Otto Sattler and Kurt Maier, a legendary duo from the bars of Prague, stood behind the stage. They were smoking cigarettes whose value in Theresienstadt I could not yet understand. I introduced myself as a guitar player from Berlin, and they offered me a smoke. We began to talk. My two celebrity colleagues explained the comedy they had to perform in the camp, self-organized entertainment for the working people of Theresienstadt, ordered by the camp administration.

Everyone who was still able to do hard labor was paid with proprietary money: ghetto crowns. They could also apply for strictly rationed tickets for their amusement – for theater, opera or for an hour at the coffee house, at the cabaret, or music. If they ordered a cup of herbal tea, the "customers" had to pay for it with the ghetto money they had "earned"!

Sattler went next door and got a guitar – there wasn't a shortage of them. A lot of inmates who were musicians had brought their beloved instruments with them. My own guitar was in the *Rosita Bar* waiting for my dad to pick it up, which he actually did.

I wanted to show Maier and Sattler my chops, so I played *Honeysuckle Rose*. Like most of my well-known colleagues I immediately forgot the surroundings and the circumstances as I played my instrument. Recently imprisoned, and I was already doing what I always did: making music.

As a musician it does not take long to find other musicians when you come to a new place. In the camp this proved to be a decisive and life-saving advantage, more so as many musicians worked as cooks. I got to meet one of them the very next day: Franta Goldschmidt, who also played guitar for a group called The Ghetto Swingers. He told me that the band could not perform right now because Vicky Werfel, their *bubenik* – the Czech word for drummer – had been put on the train for Auschwitz a couple of days ago. I told him I could play the drums. A few minutes later I had a new job; I was the *bubenik* in one of the hottest, high-octane jazz ensembles of the entire German Reich.

After this surprise Goldschmidt proceeded to offer me a Czech dumpling made from yeast dough. My stomach was used to the kind of food I ate when I spent my time on Grosse Hamburger Strasse, not this Czech dumpling. I lay in my bunk for three days in the Hanover-Barracks, or to be more exact, in barracks "B-IV."

From my privileged perch I quickly learned about the different ways people tried to cope and about what worked in camp. There was hunger and endless misery in the illusory world that was Theresienstadt; the people were emaciated and dying. Meals consisted of meager rations of bread, carrot peels or millet soup, flour dumplings and, every once in a long while, some vegetables. Meat was not on the menu. Many Orthodox Jews only ate bread and potatoes as the camp administration did not provide kosher meals. Their position was: "It's your own fault!" If you did not get any food packages from home, you had to learn to adapt to what the camp had to offer in order to survive.

As a musician, a friend of cooks and being the nestling among them, things were relatively easy for me. Franta Goldschmidt and the others got me back on my feet quickly by slipping me special rations. I also managed to avoid working in the fields, making clothes or war materiel – being an indispensable "tool" in this game. I put together my everyday life in the camp, suppressed any thought of another life and accepted the conditions of this new world with all its ups and

A poster for The Ghetto Swingers

downs, with glimpses of hell but also with cabaret, theater and music.

I visited my grandparents every day, without thinking about how macabre this sort of "family life" was. Two months later they were put onto the train to Auschwitz-Birkenau and died in the gas a few days afterwards.

Meanwhile, we Ghetto Swingers stood on the stage of the coffee house and played forbidden American hot jazz from Count Basie to Duke Ellington. Our signature song was Gershwin's incomparable *I Got Rhythm,* rather fittingly.

The Ghetto Swingers were founded by the Czech engineer and amateur trumpet player Eric Vogel. His permit to form a camp combo was granted on January 8, 1943, by the Department of *Freizeitgestaltung* (department of leisure time activities) of the Jewish self-administration after some of the best musicians in Europe had arrived in Theresienstadt, among them the Prague jazz combo Weiss. The band was led by the twenty-five year old clarinet player Fricek (Fritz) Weiss. Initiatives like this were not just tolerated, they were encouraged as they fulfilled their intended role for later use as propaganda.

Being a member of The Ghetto Swingers was an iffy business. Despite some everyday advantages, it did not guarantee survival. Using self-initiative, these inmates built their own world. The audience, however, was conscripted; the lies about the "paradise" of Theresienstadt were organized perfectly.

Inmates like us, active artists of all kinds, were probably the easiest for the SS administration to submit to the collective deception. Art, theater and music provided a direct, simple and comfortable escape from the horrific everyday life in the camp. All that was needed were the items the inmates had brought along anyway: their talent and their tools of the trade. I was a poster child. When I played I forgot where I was. The world seemed in order, the suffering of people around me disappeared – life was beautiful. Nothing was further from my mind than the wall that enclosed the camp, the emaciated men, women and children, the trains to the extermination camp of Auschwitz-Birkenau. We were a "normal" band who played for a "normal" audience. We knew everything and forgot everything the moment we played a few bars. We performed for ourselves and to save our lives – like everyone else in this "town," this cruel, phony stage set for theater plays, children's operas, cabarets, scientific lectures, athletic events – an absurd social life and a bizarre, self-administrated survival in the waiting line of the ovens of the Third Reich.

Among several new inmates of the camp was Martin Roman, who arrived in January of 1944 from the Dutch transit camp Westerbork. He had to sweep the streets for the first couple of days until Eric Vogel and Paul Libensky, coordinators of the Friezeitgestaltung, recognized him: he was the former pianist of the legendary Weintraub's Syncopators who had accompanied Louis Armstrong, Coleman Hawkins, Lionel Hampton, Sydney Bechet and Django Reinhardt. They requested that he become the bandleader of The Ghetto Swingers.

Right away Roman reorganized our band along the lines of an American Big Band and came up with a formation consisting of three violins, three saxophones, four trumpets and guitar, accordion, bass and me on drums. Roman accompanied his own compositions and arrangements on piano and added a special attraction from time to time: a trio of singers in the style of the Andrews Sisters as well as the tenor Fredy Haber. We played our most popular and perhaps most appropriately named arrangement with this formation, *Avant de Mourir* (Before Dying), a tango by Georges Boulanger.

Thanks to my new friends, I got another rare privilege. At first I had lived in a huge room in the Hanover Barracks that was overflowing with people due to the three-tiered bunk beds. I had to hide my few possessions under my mattress. It was usually impossible to keep others from stealing a piece of bread and a small packet of sugar: three days' rations. I couldn't get much rest, even at night, because somebody was always awake, talking or screaming in his sleep.

One day Walter Jockel, a butcher and a fan of mine, had a surprise waiting for me in his kitchen, a large extra ration of beef – but it was not for me to eat. I could use it to get a *kumbal*, a small attic closet in one of the other barracks by using the meat to "buy" it from the supervisor. The "previous owner" had been deported to Auschwitz-Birkenau. Once again, with the help of music I could live alone, a real privilege. Alone at last, in a tiny, bug-ridden room, I lay awake at night, trying to understand what was happening to us. I only knew one thing: I wanted to stay alive, and that meant I had to go along with the system. It was the only chance I had, and that was the way most of the inmates survived: to submit to be forced to commit unacknowledged wrongful deeds which, when questioned, would become unbearable; to struggle; to keep your head down; to grab every chance to stay alive one more day; to forget that tomorrow might never come; to repress all feelings of fear or stress; to pretend and laugh away in brief, deceptive situations that resembled "normal" life. I knew that it wasn't real, but I did not have the feeling I was doing anything wrong. How can anyone say it is wrong to want to stay alive?

To later question this behavior, after these images and experiences of horror, is the legacy of those days. You are always alone with those thoughts for as long as you live. Chosen by luck and fate like everyone who survived; borne down by fate like everyone who had to suffer it.

In December of 1943, the "beautification" of Theresienstadt got underway. Work groups laid out playgrounds, the barracks lining the main streets were renovated, rose bushes were planted and the "shops" were fitted with window displays. The official program was expanded, a culture began to blossom that had been prohibited in the Reich for several years. The International Red Cross had announced it would inspect Theresienstadt. The National Socialists could not ignore this demand. They didn't want to. To the contrary – finally, the plan that lingered behind the model camp would be fulfilled.

The propaganda strategists and the administration prepared everything in minute and cruel detail. Step one was to transport around seven thousand old and sick inmates to Auschwitz-Birkenau to assure a certain "youthfulness" in the camp. After that the "beautified" image of the camp was completed by grotesque facilities such as a bank for the ridiculous ghetto currency. The streets and the simple pathways were washed with soapy water, the windows facing the street were decorated with colorful curtains and the third tiers of the beds were taken down. After all, they had made enough room.

Theater and cabaret ensembles had to rehearse select scenes of different plays, a choir consisting of almost a hundred singers prepared Verdi's *Requiem,* and we and Karel Ancerl's violin orchestra had to study a special program to perform at the "city park" – in a wooden pavilion built especially for us – from the *Bugle Call Rag* to *Bei mir bist du schön* to a jazz arrangement of Hoffmeister and Krása's children's opera written in Prague that later became an international hit, *Brundibár.*

Theresienstadt was converted into a Potemkin village: the deception of the committee of the International Red Cross was an incomprehensible success. Camp life disappeared beneath a large cloak of dead bodies smelling of roses. Not even a hint of suffering and misery could be found anywhere. Wherever the visiting committee went, they saw actors rehearsing or acting in a play before a cheering, well provided for audience. As soon as they left the scene was interrupted and "normal" conditions were reinstated. We had hoped that the Red Cross delegation would see through the charade when they interviewed inmates individually and learned the true magnitude of the horror. But far from it. Maybe they did not want to know the truth in detail?

These macabre productions were a dress rehearsal for an infamous film titled *Der Führer schenkt den Juden eine Stadt* (The Führer Gives a City to the Jews). I have never been able to understand how anyone could believe that the Nazis themselves came up with this title. In 1989 a researcher from the Netherlands, Karel Magry, proved that in fact it had a different original title, no less cynical than the other title: *Theresienstadt – ein Dokumentarfilm aus dem jüdischen Siedlungsgebiet* (Theresienstadt – A Documentary Film about the Jewish Resettlement). I presume the title was the result of a typical Jewish joke. The fact that it was simply accepted without question for so long tells us something about how much remains to be reexamined before we can come to terms with certain events of the past. There are various similar examples of the special Jewish black humor in the cabaret programs of the camp, such as the bitter chansons and cabaret songs of Manfred Greifenhagen and Leo Strauss: "*Theresienstadt, Theresienstadt/ ist da modernste Ghetto, das die Welt heut' hat*" (Theresienstadt, Theresienstadt/ is the most modern ghetto the world has). They stand as a testament to the acid test that everybody in the camp was exposed to.

At the beginning of 1944, shortly after the arrival of Martin Roman, the actor, former comedian and operetta tenor Kurt Gerron was brought from Westerbork to Theresienstadt. He became a celebrity in 1928 when he played Tiger Brown in the premiere of Brecht and Weill's *Dreigroschenoper* (The Three-

Closing Time for the House Elders
Saturday 15 – 17, 1944. Westg.-3

HERMAN'S COLLECTION, TEREZÍN MEMORIAL, COURTESY ZUZANA DVOŘÁKOVÁ

penny Opera). In 1930 he played the magician Kiepert in the movie *Der Blaue Engel* (The Blue Angel) with Emil Jennings and Marlene Dietrich, the high point of his career. He also acted together with Theo Lingen, Heinz Rühmann, Hans Albers and Hans Moser in movies like *Die Drei von der Tankstelle* (The Three from the Filling Station) and *Varieté* (Vaudeville). His career, however, took a decisive and macabre turn. In return for sparing his life, being a director and expert at spectacles, he was engaged to direct a script that had been written in 1943 about the comfortable life of the Jews in Theresienstadt – while "German soldiers risked their lives for them at the front".

The film featured everything the Nazis' cruel cynicism had to offer. And that was a lot: crowd scenes with up to seventeen thousand smiling extras, an entire city transformed into a sugarcoated stage set, a camp as an amusement park.

Everyone who participated in the production was promised their freedom. The sunny images showed the hopeful smiles of girls who were walking towards the fields with a song on their lips, their families who did some shopping, went to the bank, supervised the children at the playground or watched a soccer match. SS camp commander Rahm was engaged in a lively discussion with the children who were instructed to be complaining about the food. "Uncle Rahm, why do we have to eat sardines again?"

The Ghetto Swingers sat in the pavilion and fired up the cheering audience. We had to wear tuxedos. Some of us, myself among them, had already been issued one. There was not enough eveningwear to go around, but we all got brand new white shirts with the Star of David attached. The visual problem presented by our worn-out shoes was solved by putting a row of flowerpots up in front of us and with bandstands featuring our logo, most fitting for a popular combo. Select young men displayed naked torsos and swayed their hammers to the music of Offenbach and "made something of themselves"; smartly dressed mothers read to their children from books from the truly comprehensive camp library. Kurt Gerron himself stepped in front of the camera: in front of two thousand spectators he recited the *Macky Messer Song* (Mack the Knife) on an open-air stage of the camp.

Everyone who participated was assured they would receive special rations and food packages even though they knew where they were coming from: the camp inmates of Theresienstadt were permitted to have a limited correspondence with relatives at home. These messages could not exceed twenty-five words without special permission and could not contain anything negative; mostly it was limited to a pre-printed form letter: "I gratefully confirm the reception of your package from . . ." including a request to send the next package. The camp administration was only too pleased that the families reacted promptly to these requests since they knew how to exploit this situation. Selected prisoners had to write pre-dated letters and ask for more packages. By the time the packages arrived, the recipients would already be dead.

ADDRESSED TO: Dr. Botmann Family, copy address E. Koter/Berlin Wittenau/Hermsdorferstrasse 50

July 31, 1944

My dear parents, today I received your card from July 11. I was very happy to get it and particularly happy to hear about Jürgen. Have you received news from our grandparents? I have received all of their mail. Everything you sent has reached me, also the other news from the eleventh. The contents were very good. How is Tullio doing? I am working with my colleagues. It often reminds me of the *Rosita Bar*. Don't be worried about me, I am doing very well. I hope that you are doing as

The Ghetto Swingers, conducted by Martin Roman, included:
Coco Schumann, drums; Fricek (Fritz) Weiss, clarinet; Fritz Goldschmidt, guitar; Nettl, accordion;
Ratner, violin; J. Taussig, trombone; and others.
From the film by Kurt Gerron: *Theresienstadt – A Documentary Film about the Jewish Resettlement*
FILM STILL, COLLECTION OF YAD VASHEM

Coco Schumann playing drums with The Ghetto Swingers
FILM STILL, COLLECTION OF YAD VASHEM

well as I am. To you, sweet Mom, all my best for your birthday even though this is late. I hope I can tell you in person. Now dear Papa, Mom and Jürgen, a thousand kisses and greetings, Heinz.

Heinz Schumann, Theresienstadt, Protectorate, Main Street, 1

On the evening of August 30, 1944, Hans Werner Kleve and his band were once again playing "our music" in Berlin at the *Café Leon* on the Lehniner Platz.

Fricek (Fritz) Weiss, clarinet FILM STILL, COLLECTION OF YAD VASHEM

A tattered shoe hidden by the bandstand, filmed by Kurt Gerron
This is but one example of how Gerron captured small details to betray the Nazis' film as propoganda.
FILM STILL, COLLECTION OF YAD VASHEM

The slate board clapped for the last shots of the promotional film about Theresienstadt, which was never completed for theatrical distribution in cinemas. A
new, more authentic wind was blowing, following the forced lightheartedness
of the days filled with joyous music. The number of concerts fell drastically, the
"beautification" of the camp turned to dust. The showcase city of Theresienstadt
had served its purpose for the visit by the International Red Cross and the film.
The events of the war, of which we did not catch much, seemed to set in motion
unexpected changes that required radical decisions to be made. The mood of

the camp administration turned edgy and tense. We sensed the growing anxiety of the SS. Sometimes we overheard bits of conversation and the rumor mill went into high gear. All of us wanted to believe we were going to be freed. But we would have been just as happy to be liberated by the "enemy". By then every child there knew that hope could save lives, just as despair could kill. Our hopes and illusions were so specific that we made plans for our careers once the war was over.

On September 23 after the evening service for Yom Kippur, the most sacred Jewish holiday, the Jewish elder Dr. Eppstein, on behalf of the camp commander, announced the beginning of the *Arbeitseinsatztransporte nach Osten* (work crew transports to the East). There was our reward: deportation to Auschwitz-Birkenau. Right up to the end we had clung to the belief that we could believe what the administration and the guards had promised. Now we learned better. A good thirty thousand people, among them seven thousand children, would begin their final journey during the next weeks.

The transports began on September 28, 1944. The day before, we gathered in front of the posted lists and looked for our names with an indescribable feeling in our stomachs. Exactly two thousand four hundred and ninety-nine people were on the lists posted on the first day, and the chaos that followed was accordingly. Kurt Gerron was one of the first to find his name on the list. Before the film shoot had been completed, he had been dismissed as director. Someone explained to me later that he had fallen on his knees in front of the camp commander and begged for his life: "But I made your film!" It did not help. While the film was being edited in Prague in the winter of 1944-45, Gerron and his wife had already been murdered in Auschwitz-Birkenau. Neither celebrity nor service to country could help anymore. From now on we were all the same. Nothing helped, not even having an essential position in the camp. The entire camp apparatus was drastically downsized.

Even Fricek Weiss and I found our names on the list. The next day we boarded the train together with two thousand five hundred others, the first train of the *Arbeitseinsatztransporte nach Osten*. When the famous composer Translateur had to climb into a boxcar the guards were whistling one of his most famous melodies, the wildly popular *Sportpalast Walzer*, not knowing who was in front of them.

The floor of the freight car was covered by a thin layer of old straw; we sat on it, crammed together, next to and on top of each other. The stench was overwhelming. We were lucky we were on our way a few hours after they had loaded

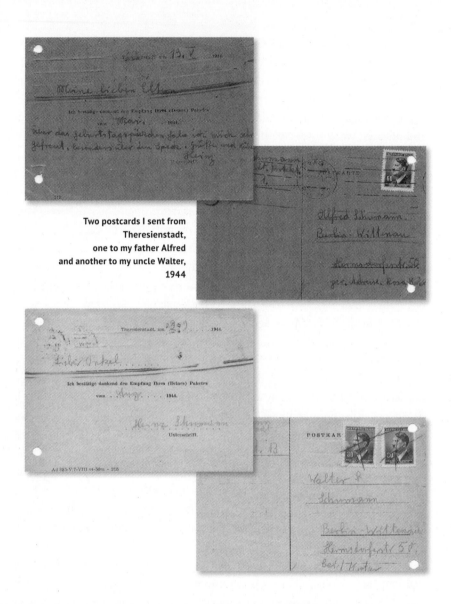

Two postcards I sent from
Theresienstadt,
one to my father Alfred
and another to my uncle Walter,
1944

us into the box cars, and not – as happened often – with the train "waiting" for one or two days at the "railway station" of Theresienstadt.

Nevertheless, people jammed together next to me began to die the first day, from hunger, from disease, from despair – a quiet death, unnoticed by most of us. We were in a daze. We only moved to get some relief from the pain in our extremities, or – at first – to make our difficult way to an overflowing bucket that stood in the corner. I accidentally stepped on an old man trying to get to the bucket. He did not move. He was not alive anymore. For how long was hard to determine – minutes, hours, nobody knew. The noise of the train was so deafening we could not hear the sounds of life or the sounds of dying.

In the afternoon I managed to push up against the boxcar door, which was open just a crack – a very much sought-after spot because of the fresh air. The train slowed down again, and I looked out, trying to recognize something. I could hardly believe my eyes. The place we were rolling through seemed familiar. The freight train wasn't traveling due east, it was making a fairly large detour. The outer districts of my hometown were passing by: Schlachtensee, Grunewald – it was Berlin out there!

I took heart, stood up, climbed over to the SS-man who was standing next to the crack in the door and said in a strong Berlin accent: *"Icke muesst' mal austreten, könnt' icke hier wohl mal rauspinkeln?"* ("I have to relieve myself, can I pee out from here?") He granted my request and let me get closer to the crack. The train slowed down again, the railroad lines had been bombed heavily around Berlin. Slowly it rolled into the Halensee, my old stomping grounds, like it wanted to drop me off at home.

Back then, thousands of boxcars had rattled past our windows, and I never had thought once about what they were transporting. Now I was rolling past my old apartment. The perspective had changed significantly. When I saw our old apartment building on the Kronprinzendamm and the windows of our old apartment, I almost lost it. I saw my family in front of me again, I saw flashes from my childhood. For a short time the journey to a more than uncertain future was a journey into the past. If I had lost my youth in Theresienstadt, this was the moment I became an adult. I knew something was over. Whatever happened, whatever our final destination would mean for us, I did not know. But I began to understand.

The first stop was Oranienburg. There, we spent two days in the nearby camp of Sachsenhausen, then we rattled on in a southeasterly direction until we got to our final destination. The train stopped at dawn on October 3, 1944, the doors were opened, loud voices were yelling orders. Finally our own doors slid open, we gasped for fresh air, climbed over the dead bodies among us and got out – and stood on the ramp of Auschwitz-Birkenau.

La Paloma

THE LINE OF PEOPLE moved slowly alongside the boxcars; I turned and looked around. A pungent stench hung heavily in the air. Tall smokestacks stood at some distance, towering over facilities that evidently were putting out a lot of heat because flames would shoot out of them. While I was mulling over what was being manufactured in the largest death camp in National Socialist Germany, Fricek and I walked past a group of inmates in prisoner's garb who took away all of our sparse belongings that we had with us. When they had finished we were led, stark naked, to the front end of the platform.

I stood there in front of the camp doctor, a man whose name I only learned later on: Josef Mengele. He asked me how old I was. As if someone has whispered the answer into my ear, I suddenly knew what I had to say. I stood at attention, and put my hands on my non-existing trouser seams and said: "Twenty, sir!" He looked at me with cold eyes and asked the next question: "Occupation?" I looked him directly in the eye: "Plumber and pipe layer, *Herr Hauptsturmführer!*" He indicated me to go to the right, the side where the younger and apparently healthier prisoners were. Opposite of us a crowd of old, sick and famished people gathered. I did not know *what* it meant, but I knew it meant *something*.

Shortly after that Fricek Weiss joined us, his parents standing behind him were sent to the other side by Mengele. I do not know how well Fricek understood the situation or whether it was decisive for what he did. He could not stand to be separated from them. He went back to Mengele who had sorted them out like they were new or used clothing and said to him: "*Herr Hauptsturmführer*, you sent my parents to the other side. Please, may I go with them?" Even today I can still see Mengele's grin. "But of course you may!" Fricek Weiss, our Benny Goodman, ran over to them, to the other side. I was shoved and pushed forwards and I lost sight of him, wondering about the ashes that drifted through the air and covered the ground of the entire area.

After the guards had marched us into the entry area of the camp, we had to stop and stand at attention in front of an electrified fence. A gruesome sight. Burned bodies were hanging inside the barbed wire. Machine guns were pointed at us and the electric current was shut off; a gang of prisoners began its work. They pried open the stiff fingers of the charred hands and took the dead bodies down from the fence. Mere routine. A ritual we would be watching every morning – provided we did not decide to "go into the wire", like those who could not bear to live another day. After the fence had been cleared, the electricity was turned on again and we continued our march.

Our transport group waited for the SS and their attack dogs in the thinly populated "E" camp – only new prisoners who had arrived before us from Theresienstadt were held there. The camp commander stood in front of them and told us how it was: "So, you pig Jews, just so you know: you are in the Auschwitz-Birkenau death camp. You already know the way in, the way out is over there." He pointed at the smoke billowing from the smokestacks. That was the explanation. The stench, the ashes, the other side – Fricek, his parents, my grandparents. Now I understood.

We were assigned to the barracks, which were converted horse stables with wooden bunk beds to sleep on. At the entrance, our heads were shaved. Curiously, we were not tattooed like everyone who came from Theresienstadt. I was able to regain my composure somewhat when our group of starved, naked men stood in line waiting to be registered. I played the same game I had played at the ramp. Standing at attention, looking them right in the eye. "Twenty, *Herr Sturmbannführer!* Of course I can work. Plumber and pipe layer!" He looked at me rather astonished considering the combination of a Berlin lip and an honorable trade.

My guardian angel seemed to take an interest in me again that very same afternoon. A man who was dressed well compared to the prison garb we were wearing walked up to me, stopped and asked: "Say, are you the guy from Berlin?" I stood at attention. "*Jawoll, Herr Blockältester!*" "Man, Coco. Knock it off! It's me – Heinz!" At first I did not know who he was, then he explained. Heinz Herrig. The croupier from Berlin had been to the *Rosita Bar* numerous times and was a huge fan of Tullio and his band. He knew the music of the *Maier-Sattler Duo,* and I introduced him to Otto Sattler, who had also been assigned to our barracks.

Heinz immediately came up with a plan. There are bands in Auschwitz, just like in Theresienstadt. Until recently, thirty thousand Sinti, Roma and other gypsies had been stationed here, men, women and children. The "E" block was called the gypsy block before inmates from Theresienstadt arrived. Then the camp administration had to accommodate the prisoners from the Theresienstadt transport on short notice, so they herded all of the "E" camp inmates into the gas. Heinz told us the kapos had to use batons to drive the terrified women and children down from the ceiling rafters where they had tried to hide in terror. So only a few days ago, a band had played in these barracks over which a gruesome silence had descended, a gypsy band made up of thirty musicians.

Heinz thought this was our chance to stay alive for now. He presented us to the *Lagerälteste* (camp elder) as musicians. The camp elders had a special position. They were prisoners like us, but as a rule they were "authentic" Germans – prisoners who had been brought here from Sachsenhausen starting in 1940, "professional criminals" of every kind. They had a relatively free hand and sometimes exercised their power over the Jewish prisoners out of fear for their own lives, but sometimes also without. One of them was a sadistic killer. After getting up in the morning he would beat one, two, three Jews to death, just like that, for the fun of it. This was fine with the SS. Some of the camp elders had their own band, among other things, as a sign of their status.

It was also usually not a problem to get an instrument at Auschwitz as some of the arriving musicians had managed to bring them along until they were taken away at the infamous ramp by the so-called Canada commando. This command, the same one that had "greeted" us, consisted of privileged inmates who collected everything the arriving prisoners had brought with them and transported the confiscated property to one of thirty warehouses. These rooms, filled with mountains of personal effects from what can be called the prisoners' last luggage, were called "Canada" because, for Poles, the country was the epitome of wealth and riches. The prisoners in that command understood how to turn their work to their own advantage by putting aside some of the loot to use later for barter inside the camp.

Our camp elder had just lost his gypsy band, and he immediately agreed to Heinz's proposal. Heinz led us to the hall where the instruments were stored among other items and said: "Look around, it's all there." I chose a Selmer guitar made by a French company that had also made guitars for Django Reinhardt. I had never played on such a fine instrument before. I did not think about the previous owner – it was the only way. I had gotten used to the disappearance and murder of people, as much as I could ever get used to something like this.

Rather intuitively and because of the shock of the past few days, I sensed I could not afford any further sentimentalities. There was one and only one principle that mattered here: "Every man for himself." In this context, it also meant becoming a small part of the rampant inhumanity. If I did not want to die in this death camp, I had to focus on saving my life at the expense of humaneness and feeling.

So Otto Sattler and I wound up playing music again on our first evening in Auschwitz – in front of the camp elder, a professional criminal with a taste for folksy music. We played songs from the *Reeperbahn*, the famous red light district in Hamburg and Paul Lincke songs, all at his request. He grabbed a chair and two sticks and drummed along with the music – just as I had done when I was four, at the home of my grandparents.

One of the next transports from Theresienstadt brought Martin Roman and Eric Vogel. We immediately set about planning a band led by Roman. It was easy to convince the camp elder. They all competed to have the best camp band. The SS did not do anything to interrupt the competition. They applauded the performances. A lot of them even liked the music – they had grown up at the same time, in the same environment, with the same influences as I had. The difference that separated us was made clear to me in a horrible way that day at school at the blackboard, but it did not have anything to do with music. We musicians were a welcome "diversion" from the monotonous, gray, "lethal" boredom of daily life in the camp, and we quickly became an essential part of this macabre world.

Roman got the musicians who had come from Theresienstadt together and founded his band. If a matching instrument could not be found the musicians received another and had to fake their skill as best they could because their life might depend on it. Eric Vogel could not find a trumpet. We gave him a mandolin and made sure our dangerous audience would not notice anything. The difference between Theresienstadt and Auschwitz was very clear to us. It was the difference between living in the naive hope of being set free and trying to stay alive for the next couple of hours.

Next door in the "D" block, a band played that either cynically named or had to name itself *Wesola Piatka* (The Happy Five). We could not make contact, except talking briefly through a fence when both bands were performing open-air concerts.

After a few weeks we were not required to play only for private "amusements"; instead, we were integrated into the "official" camp routine like the other bands. By now we had earned some privileges, received special rations and did not have to live in the common barracks sharing a bunk bed with six or seven other inmates. The pecking order in the camp became established among the prisoners with time. Any resistance to the camp and block elder, who were bosom buddies with the SS pack, resulted in paying with your life. Nobody had the will or the strength to object to the privileges of a few prisoners like us. Whoever did not get an extra ration, whoever did not have his bowl filled from the bottom of the soup pot was soon done for and lost weight until his bones stuck out. Whoever walked around like a *Muselmann* (Muslim), as they called the walking skeletons, would be sent to the gas chamber in a couple of days.

We were in a privileged situation not just because we were musicians and artists but because of our previous stay at Theresienstadt. It was not clear why this was the case. Any prisoner from Theresienstadt could be sent to the gas chambers, but not one of us was ever tattooed. Apparently somebody thought they could use us for barter. After all, prisoners from the "model concentration camp" had a certain fame; we heard rumors that in some cases sums going into the millions were flowing for inmates in order to buy their freedom.

Heinz told me about a kind of family camp for arrivals from Theresienstadt where children were reportedly being spoiled with chocolate. But then the entire group, men, women, children, was sent into the gas. There was no apparent logic to the way the Nazis acted. Maybe there wasn't any. This was dangerous because one could not increase the odds of survival by scheming or predictability. Arbitrariness and randomness reigned.

We musicians were better off than the others in various ways. A private single bed came at a price, however. Every morning began with the order: "Band, everybody out!" If we were not playing for the SS while they tattooed the new arrivals, we usually had to be at the camp's main gate. This is where the work crews or the "selected" prisoners marched towards the gas chambers located at some distance from the camp.

So each morning brought the horror once again: a long line of emaciated people on their last journey. I kept telling myself that it was not the music's fault. If music does not save your life, at least it saves the present day.

Man is a peculiar invention. Unpredictable and ruthless. The images I saw in those days were unbearable and yet, we had to bear them. We provided the music, to save our skin. We were playing music in hell.

One of the favorite songs of the Nazi henchmen was *La Paloma* (The Dove) from the Hans Albers film *Grosse Freiheit Nr. 7* (Great Freedom Number 7). We sat at the main gate of the death camp playing this song about longing, about the sea, the stars and the happiness of freedom: *"A wind blows from the south and carries me out to sea. My child, do not be sad, farewell is always painful . . ."*

When they walked past us towards the gas chambers, the children looked me directly in the eye. They knew exactly where they were going. These images are burned into my mind. I can blink as much as I want. Sometimes it helps when tears start running down my cheek, but as soon as I open my eyes the image returns. Something inside of me has been broken forever, something that can never be repaired.

In the evening, we played for the camp elder and his colleagues and the SS, at small banquets with food, vodka, German Möve cigarettes and singing. We played requests from Linke's *Glühwürmchen* (Glow Little Glow Worm) and the hit song *Eine Nacht voller Seligkeit* (A Night Full of Bliss) to *You Are My Lucky Star*. We were in a constant state of stress to fulfill their wishes in minute detail. One mistake, a whim, a careless gesture could have meant the immediate death sentence for one or all of us. Every "successful" performance, however, bought us another day, provided essential advantages – and because of it, we tolerated quite a lot of things. At times the "rewards" were absurd. The camp's tailor shop had to make dark blue blazers for us, made to measure, with a small golden lyre stitched to our lapels!

A very special evening of "entertainment" took place in the infamous delousing showers. By invitation of the camp elders. They wore the dresses taken from women who had walked past us that morning and got plastered drunk. They kept requesting songs over and over. The evening ended with them ordering us to drink champagne with them – from "their" women's shoes.

I got a bad case of dysentery with colic and was sent to the hospital block running a high fever. Suddenly a kapo came up to my bunk and hissed at me: "You've got to get out right now!" He had learned that new transports were arriving, in which case they had to make room in the camp. The hospital block was always the first place they started. Ten minutes after his warning, I was standing in front of the door, weak and staggering, the first trucks arrived. The SS was "cleaning up".

One morning not too long after that Otto Sattler was standing at the fence of our camp looking onto Main Street. Heinz Herrig had told us that another transport had arrived from Theresienstadt. Sometimes we had the opportunity to look for familiar faces, undetected by the guards. As he did every morning, Dr. Mengele sent most of the arrivals down Main Street that morning, from the loading ramp directly to the gas chambers.

Suddenly Sattler froze. His wife and his five children were walking past him. Separated only by a fence they looked at each other for the last time; the horrific stream of the "selected" prisoners moved forward relentlessly. Otto watched them as they went but could do nothing. He knew what they were only beginning to suspect.

That evening we were playing again in front of our camp elder. When Otto could not keep back his tears, the camp elder growled at him: "Why are you crying all the time – it spoils the mood in here!" Otto explained what had happened but did not make much of an impression. "Well, that's no reason to cry. After all, you're going to be joining them soon enough!" We were deeply shaken, but we kept on playing, minute by minute, to prove our "usefulness".

With the duo from Holland Jonny and Jones, we also played for an infamous *SS Rottenführer* (corporal) from the political prisoner unit. Anybody in camp who had done anything wrong was sent to the bunker of this unit, and this thug used unspeakable methods to torture them to death. All of us were terrified of this monster.

He ordered us in our best outfits for an intimate performance at one of the barracks, where he sat all by himself and listened to us. After a little while he got up, walked over and sat down beside me. I felt sick. He asked me a question: "Say, you're from Berlin?" And after I nodded: "Yes? Nice. Me too. Where did you play?" I told him everything, and he listened. We talked for a while. I could not believe he was human. Only during the day when he wore his uniform would he be a beast, a stone-cold, ruthless sadist. Now he was sitting next to me chatting about music.

I finally gathered up my courage and asked: "*Herr Rottenführer*, do you think I will get out of here alive?" He paused, then answered quietly: "I don't know." He got up and said: "Kids, you played well tonight, come here!" He took us to a huge *Effektenkammer,* a stall in one of the warehouses where mountains of shoes, clothes, eyeglasses and human hair were being stored. Tidy and sorted. Haunting. He stood in front of a mountain of thousands of shoes and told us to take our pick, our pay. This evening was an internal inferno, but music once again saved my life and the lives of others. At least it made it more bearable. Without shoes it was very hard to survive. Whoever had a pair of shoes did not take them off when going to sleep because they would be gone the next morning for sure.

The approaching winter brought along its own hardship. At five in the morning, we had to report for roll call. Whoever didn't have any shoes had to stand for hours in freezing slush up to their ankles. Many of the arrivals who had been deported from Hungary had wrapped their feet in newspapers and did not have much of a chance to survive this torment. Either they came down with the flu or pneumonia, suffering for a few days, or they froze to death on the spot.

In November of 1944, the gassings were cut back but continued until January of 1945 – murders and dying continued incessantly. Most of the concentration camp prisoners were at the end of their rope. During this period I tried to pray sometimes. My life up until then had not exactly been religious, I had not really dealt with existential problems before. But here in this hell, life was quickly reduced to them. Even in Theresienstadt I had not cared about being Jewish; here I slowly learned to accept it. A better way to put it would be to say that the Nazis had hammered this fact into me, and now I embraced my heritage in a very special manner. Every time we sat at the main gate and the other prisoners made their way past us to their deaths, I prayed to God and begged: "Do something, anything! Come down and help these people!" But nobody came. Nothing happened. No answer. Everyone in the concentration camp prayed to God, each to his own. Their prayers went mostly unanswered. There they frolicked above the clouds, stepping on each other's toes, the Christian and the Jewish God, Allah and Buddha. But when we needed them, nobody came.

I learned a few things during those hours. For one thing, nothing stinks as badly as human flesh. For another, that I was a Jew. Despite everything that happened, I did find faith that did not involve a particular God in heaven. Since then I know there is "something" out there and that this "something" saved me. There simply could not be as many coincidences as I had experienced. But to this day I still do not know *what* it was. In any case, it is not a God I can visit in a church, rather, a somewhat different being, a guardian angel.

In December the rate of change in the camp picked up. Some of the smokestacks had not been blowing smoke for two or three weeks, and the first crematoriums were being dismantled. In January the main crematoriums were blown up. I found out later that Himmler had ordered it.

One morning in January of 1945, Heinz came to me and said: "We're going on transport!" Nobody knew if this was a good thing. We were afraid with good reason that the march through the main gate would lead directly to our deaths. When we reported for roll call the next morning, we were given a ration of bread, then we were led off in the direction of the gas chambers. What kind of perverted game had they thought up this time?

Nobody played music at the gate because the "E" Block with thirty thousand inmates was being cleared. When the front end of the column of inmates turned away from the gas chambers and marched towards the ramp, many of us were dazed by the tension of the moment. We were actually loaded into the boxcars of several endlessly long trains. Once again – I couldn't believe it – the trains headed for Berlin. Like before, we spent one or two days in Oranienburg and then headed south. This time I was not able to get close to the crack in the door, but I seemed to feel our old apartment building passing by without knowing whether it was still standing. How long ago had it been? Not very long, but an eternity all the same.

Our destination was Kaufering, a satellite camp of Dachau, one of the first concentration camps the Nazis had built north of Munich in 1933 – the year I would have given anything to join the Jungvolk.

The arrival in Kaufering reminded me of Auschwitz-Birkenau. My guardian angel had flown ahead of me. The camp elder was Jirka Taussig, the former trombone player of The Ghetto Swingers. We greeted each affectionately, and right away I was given a special ration from the kitchen to get me halfway back on my feet. Kaufering was not set up to be a death camp, but the misery we had to endure here was horrible as well. Instead of barracks we were put into shallow, roofed, earth-covered dugouts with the floor covered with old, rotting straw. We slept packed closely together. Every morning started with an inspection to see if the person sleeping next to you was still alive. The dead were brought outside; the resulting space was occupied again. The conditions were catastrophic.

I clung to my life. Music helped me here, too. The word spread quickly that I was a musician. A prisoner who was in the *Aussenkommandos* (exterior work detail), laying cables and working on farms, had discovered an old, derelict guitar in a barn. Taussig managed to slip a bar of margarine out of the kitchen, and the next day the prisoner asked the farmer whether he would like to trade. He smuggled the big thing past the guards into camp – unbelievable. Unfortunately, it did not have strings on it. The *Aussenkommandos* got hold of some pieces of cable. I removed the insulation, tensioned them and tightened the cables. I was able to bring the guitar back to life, and it didn't sound too bad.

From then on I played small regular kitchen concerts and got paid with an extra portion of food, which kept me going. The music was an emotional nourishment for my fellow inmates; it may have preserved the optimism of one or the other among them. In this situation we all waited, kept our heads down, simply endured. By then we all knew that the path to the end of the "Thousand Year Reich" was much shorter than the path to the *Endsieg* (final victory).

Still, the next minute could be the end. The SS mob was as dangerous as in Auschwitz-Birkenau. One morning during roll call, a pack of dead drunk soldiers entertained themselves by dousing us with water. Many collapsed on the spot and froze to death. I got through it until the roll call had ended, then ran like the others to a nearby snow drift, took off my clothes and rubbed snow and ice all over my body until I warmed up. Our barracks contained a cast iron stove, barely heated with waste wood, but it was enough to save us that morning. A lot of prisoners in the barracks next to ours died from pneumonia over the next few days. It was what they called a "joke", a joke played by the SS, who – drunk and having a good time – laughed themselves to death watching their victims die.

Eventually I became the prefect of the infirmary, the *Stubenälteste*, the only one in this position who did not carry a rubber baton. That was not without danger because if there really were a fight in "my" block I would have been the first one to go. I did not want to be one of those guys who got respect through violence. I am not lumping them all together and judging them because I know only too well that your life often depended on it. A lot of us had to walk the fine line between victim and victimizer; the fate of a lot of prisoners was much more dramatic than mine, more inevitable. I had the unswerving intention to not become a victimizer. I was able to succeed thanks to my youth, my music and the amount of sympathy that could be mustered in situations like this. The effect was distinct and dangerous – everyone wanted to be in my hospital block. I almost got busted.

Soon all of Kaufering became a hospital camp because an epidemic of spotted fever broke out, a usually fatal disease spread by lice. The entire area was placed under quarantine, and the camp was cordoned off by guards from the outside. Anyone who tried to get in or out was shot on the spot. The meager food rations we received were tossed over the fence. Other than that we were left to our fate. The beds in the dugouts emptied fast, and the few of us not infected with the disease sprinkled chlorine on the stinking camp straw we were sleeping on. It was disgusting, but the lice who were spreading the disease thought so, too. We were spared.

We were called to assembly in April. Kaufering was being shut down. Everyone was given a blanket and half a loaf of bread. We were marched to Innsbruck. The condition of this sad group trudging southwards was indescribable. I cannot say for sure where they took us. We were in a kind of trance state, apathetic. I recall seeing a city sign that said Pasing, and that women on the streets were crying while we filed past them and tried to give us water. Our SS guards shoved them back with the butts of their rifles.

The forest began behind the city and the trail seemed endless. Suddenly a battalion of the Wehrmacht (armed forces) appeared. "Our" SS faced off with them, but the General protested that they were exposing German civilians and his courageous soldiers at the front lines to such a miserable sight. When he learned the destination and reason for our march, he was satisfied. We were on our way to join General Schörner, who had the nickname *Soldatenklau* (soldier-thief) because he took lost or sick soldiers and put them into oddball units and gave them special assignments. He had set up machine guns in a valley near Innsbruck where they intended to make short shrift of us. It would not come to that.

We arrived in Wolfratshausen on the evening of April 30, 1945 and made camp for the night on the grounds of some abandoned migrant worker's barracks. We had a bunk bed under our backs for the first time in a long while. The next morning we stepped outside and noticed to our great surprise that most of our guards had taken off; only two SS-men had decided to stay with us. They had the absurd thought that by handing us over to the Americans alive they could save their skin. Their situation was not the best. We needed a few moments to grasp what had happened. It was hard not to string them up on the spot. The other former block seniors were eager to do it. It was understandable, all of us felt some sort of satisfaction at the thought – but others and myself refused to take part in it. Overnight, we had gotten the power of life and death over our tormentors. To have reason prevail over the indescribable hate and rage was not easy.

Our "guards" wanted to get on our good side. One of them asked us to help him take off his epaulets and said, "I have always been good to you!" They actually did do us a great service, inadvertently. When some tanks suddenly appeared, they dove for cover and we did, too, following the impulse. They thought it was the Americans and were afraid for their lives. We did not understand the situation and were about to jump up and run to our deaths. They were retreating Waffen SS, and they would have killed all of us if we hadn't hit the deck in time. When we heard the rumble of tanks again the next morning, being more experienced now, one of us slipped out to have a look. He reported back: "Star on the tanks – Americans!" This was it.

An American pastor climbed out of the second tank. He kept his eyes on us as he walked towards us and started to cry. He said a quiet blessing. A Protestant preacher blessing us Jews – a touching scene.

I was free, but my freedom was compromised. I had come down with typhoid fever the past few days, and I had angina because of the nights sleeping on the ice cold. I suddenly had a high fever. I was put on a horse-drawn carriage along with several other sick prisoners and taken to a sickbay in Fährenwald. Many of them died on the way; besides me, only one person made it. During the ride he became delirious: "I'm Hitler! I'm Hitler!" he kept shouting over and over. Well, the world was shifting for me in those hours, too, because I decided I was going to continue as a musician . . .

I do not know for how long I was delirious. When the fever was at its peak, I saw a sunlit meadow, and my mom and dad were there. They looked at me and shouted: "Heinz, Heinz, Heinz!" I opened my eyes and looked right into the friendly face of a nurse who smiled down at me and said, "He made it." I had the feeling I was about to say goodbye and my parents had pulled me back. In any case, it was over now.

After bumping into the Americans – our liberators – those of us who were healthy roamed through Wolfratshausen. The streets were eerily empty. Many residents had hidden out of fear of the Americans and in minutes had abandoned their shops. My former fellow prisoners rummaged through all of the deserted rooms for the things they needed most. Somebody brought me a guitar! It helped me get my bearings while I lay in my hospital bed. As soon as I could sit up, I would play it – what else?

At the beginning of July I was back on my feet and said goodbye to the nice Hungarian nurse. I got transit papers from the Americans and climbed into a freight train for the last time in my life – destination Berlin!

I got off the train in Pankow and went to Uncle Max's garden cottage. He had escaped the Nazi stalking. When I knocked and he opened the door, he stared at me, dumbfounded. After the news that I had been taken to Auschwitz-Birkenau, everyone had assumed with great certainty I was dead. In addition, my appearance had changed: emaciated face and hair that was slowly growing back. But the initial confusion gave way to effusive joy – and when I learned that my parents were alive and already back in Berlin, I could share it without worry. My uncle organized a carriage on the spot, and we headed to Halensee. When my mother saw me she almost fainted, but I held her in my arms to let her know I was real. A little while later my dad came home from work, and I learned how they had fared.

In 1942 my dad still had the option to disassociate himself from his family, but he never considered it. The Gestapo arrested my mom in 1943 while she was buying cigarettes on the black market. She was taken to the jail on Bessemerstrasse. The following night, bombs hit the jail and set it on fire. Many prisoners died in the flames. My mom was lucky and got to safety. Badly injured, she limped to our home in the Kurfürstenstrasse. She lay in the back room where my dad took care of her. Two days later, there was a knock on the door, the Gestapo. When they asked my dad about the whereabouts of his wife, my dad answered: "You should know better than I do. After all, you arrested her." A short pause, a brief exchange of glances and a quick answer: "Then we will have to inform you that she is deceased."

This is how my dad saved the life of his wife – with an answer that showed great presence of mind. My mom was taken for dead for the time being and was out of danger. When she was halfway back on her feet, my parents decided to leave Berlin and go live with friends in Silesia. For the perilous journey, they taught my one and a half year old baby brother Jürgen to stick out his little arm and to crow "Heil Hitler" whenever he saw anyone wearing a uniform. This trick paid off on the train ride; whenever the police came by my mom pretended to be asleep and my dad gave them his ID card. Jürgen did what he had been taught to do. How could anyone wake up this tired woman and ask for her papers after the child had touched their hearts?

My mom came up with a new variation on arrival in Silesia. All of her papers had been destroyed in an air raid. In this situation, she even had the chutzpa to apply for permission to move furniture to the home of her first-born son, who was living in the protectorate of Bohemia and Moravia! For me, an inmate of Theresienstadt at that time . . . my parents were unbelievable. For the remainder of the war they lived in the woods, until the Russians liberated them and they returned to Berlin. They moved into a small apartment on Ringbahnstrasse at the Halensee train station. When I came back, my father had already improvised a small upholstery shop.

And yet, our family was not the same as it had been. Grandfather Louis and his wife had been murdered in Auschwitz-Birkenau; my favorite aunt Hanni and her husband had been killed. Two of my mom's siblings had left Germany – Arthur moved to Bolivia, Trude to England – the others had survived with a lot of luck and the help of their "Aryan" spouses. A few of my cousins, great uncles and great aunts, however, never returned.

My parents, Jürgen and I sat together again and could hardly believe it. Even today I cannot really grasp how I got out alive of that hell on Earth while millions of others had to die . . . Why them, why not me?

I got going the very next day to see what had happened to my old stomping grounds. I walked down the Kurfürstendamm, or rather where it used to be. The city was one big pile of rubble, only the streets had been half-cleared away and passable. The rows of bombed out, burned down apartment buildings were a creepy sight. It was an eerie feeling that everything here was also real – a completely different reality from the one I had known inside the hermetically sealed world of the camps. Here as well, the "Thousand Year Reich" had brought death and despair for millions of people no matter which side they were on. In a way I could feel how the hate, the rage, the despair and the resentment that had eaten so deeply into me were transforming. In the middle of this landscape of ash and rubble, in the face of pleas written with chalk on broken doorways by torn families asking for information about their lost loved ones, the starving survivors, children playing in the ruins – a very particular kind of a temporary relief from troubling thoughts began to take shape. My parents were alive, my brother was alive, many of my relatives and I – we had all survived, together with these "others", in a burned-out land. We all had met our fate and none of us had it easy. Above everything else stood one realization: we are free, life can and must go on. Everything else would sort itself out. Those thoughts went through my head as I walked down the Kurfürstendamm with eyes wide open.

On Uhlandstrasse, I discovered a sign that arose my curiosity. Some smart guy had already opened a bar, the *Ronny Bar*. I don't think anyone will be surprised by the fact that I could not just walk past that door. Bully Buhlan and a bunch of my old buddies were sitting there and played as if nothing had happened. They had assumed, like so many others, that I had died in a concentration camp. When I walked into the bar, there was a sudden silence. They looked at me like I was a ghost when I tried to greet them with a casual grin, which vacillated between cockiness and uncertainty. Then a great hullabaloo broke out. What a surprise! None of us knew how to conduct himself in this situation. After the initial storm of congratulations and welcomes an awkward moment ensued, but fortunately not for long. We understood each other without words and communicated the best way we knew how. We grabbed our instruments and started playing.

The days that followed were a deliverance for me. I explored the surroundings I had been forced to leave two years earlier while I was still a boy. I tried to forget for now the long, long time that lay in between. Three days after my return I was playing guitar at the *Ronny Bar*. I explained where I had been, but I was unable to tell them what had really happened there. Because I had survived, I could not talk about it. By now I can talk about it, but I can't recount how it really was – the experiences were too monstrous for that. Words fail. When I was asked what happened I waved it away by saying: "Theresienstadt, Auschwitz, Dachau – you wouldn't believe me anyway." I had the feeling nobody could understand what had happened. I myself could not.

Anyway, I had found my friends again, friends with whom I had spent carefree weeks, and I was happy to be with them again, the Germans. The last thing I wanted was for them to look at me and feel ashamed for what had been done to me and to others in their name.

To be honest, I felt ashamed for them: that what I had to suffer was done in my own – German – name. Only the thin layer of my Jewish identity separated me from the victimizers and had become my moral support. This led me back to the Jewish community, where I became a member once again. My religious community had not played a significant role in my childhood and adolescence. But when I stood there once again, in Berlin, my home town, still unable to grasp what I had seen and experienced in Auschwitz-Birkenau, particularly the fact that I made it out of there, I said to myself: "If they want to make me a Jew, well then – I'll be one!" Now more than ever: for one, out of my respect for all the people I had seen die in the concentration camps, the many friends and family; for another, out of defiance. I had survived, but that was coincidental. I was meant to be among the dead, one of millions. I decided to embrace my Jewish faith without properly knowing its teachings. After the days at the camp gate, I cannot believe in the God of churches. I sometimes go into the forest to think about all of this. Sometimes I encounter "Him", and we understand each other. No more – and no less.

The Neue Synagoge, severely damaged during Allied bombing
Oranienburgerstrasse, Berlin, April 1, 1948
COURTESY: BUNDESARCHIV

Summertime

T HOSE WEEKS were "electric". Later on, a television program would proclaim: "There has never been so much of a beginning!" Nobody really knew what to do, what not to do, or where to begin. People felt relief and bewilderment at the same time. Even I stood around with mixed feelings when the *Stunde Null* struck (the "zero hour" of Nazi capitulation). I owned an instrument and didn't think about anything much, but just kept on playing.

The evenings got longer that late summer because of the curfew imposed in the afternoon already – and they would not get shorter anytime soon. Right after the war ended, forbidden music gained back territory it had lost, except for tiny islands. Ever since the general prohibition of dance music following the debacle at Stalingrad, there was not enough "supply" of entertainment for people; they were addicted to dancing and to amusing themselves. They wanted to forget or repress thoughts about the horrors of the previous years at least for a few hours. Jazz and swing had survived the war years in Germany, and even though the music had been whacked, sidelined and "Germanized", it was now flourishing and once again developed its inherent freedom. All of the clubs and jazz cellars I grew up with had been reduced to ash and rubble; everywhere people were improvising. One club after another opened its doors again.

This was fine with the Allied forces. Jazz was "their" music, and they welcomed any common denominator that would increase their ability to control the extraordinary situation the Germans were in. The Armed Forces Network (AFN) studios in Berlin were continuously broadcasting all the latest hits from a mobile transmitter that was carried around on a truck.

The songs of Ella Fitzgerald, Louis Armstrong and Fats Waller were swinging across the streets lined with rubble and toppled walls; George Gershwin's *Summertime* was huge that August. Not just for us and for Germany, but a new beginning for music was underway.

Uniformed American officer and U.S. service vehicle in front of the ruins of the *Aschinger* brewpub
British sector, Kufürstendamm 26; Berlin, 1946
PHOTO: FRITZ ESCHEN, COURTESY: DEUTSCHE FOTOTEK

It was not just an "eruption" of jazz. The interruption of the past several years had left deep, indelible scars. The past could not be erased; however, it could be somewhat "postponed". During the last two years of the dictatorship we had lost essential elements of the true jazz feeling and were not able to keep up with new developments. The current assignment was to get in touch with the new directions jazz had taken – like American bebop. That wasn't easy, there was no demand for jazz from mainstream Germany. It wanted entertainment in general and popular entertainment in particular.

Many musicians could not straddle two horses at the same time and changed over to popular German music in the following years in order to make a living.

For the time being, I enjoyed some beautiful wild months of careless joy being able to play again regardless whether I played club music, jazz or anything else that was new and unusual for us. I soaked it all in and tried to catch up with what I had missed out on during the past few years. I had played with Joe Glaser at the *Groschenkeller* before, our drummer from the *Ronny Bar*. Now we were sitting in his living room listening to current hits on AFN until one of the frequent blackouts silenced the radio. We shared one of his Lucky Strikes in the dark while Joe got me up to speed, telling me stories about what was happening in the scene.

The drummer and piano player Willy Kettel asked me if I wanted to play for the Russians. One afternoon we went to the *Sommerlatte*, a small club next to the Friedrichstadt-Palast.

We played semi-improvised Russian music and tangos – for good pay: vodka and a couple of potatoes! The Russians convinced me that in order to pursue my career I needed to learn how to hold my drink, as they put us under the tables with their double and triple shots.

On the evening of August 22, 1945, I left the *Ronny Bar* feeling great, walking down the Kurfürstendamm, watching the crowds. Someone waved at me from the other side of the street. Two girls were standing there. They seemed to be very friendly; it would have been quite irresponsible to not walk over to them, so I went to say hello. I knew one of them from my youth, Bella Hirschfeld. She introduced her friend, Gertraud Goldschmidt, who knew who I was: "You were in Theresienstadt and played drums, weren't you?"

We decided to continue our conversation in her tiny flat on Dahlmannstrasse and smoked the cigarettes I had gotten for playing. Gertraud told me about her son Peter, who would be five years old the next day. His father had left them after he was born and had gone back to Hungary; he never wrote a letter or sent a package. When the deportation of the Jews began in 1942, Gertraud was able to hide her son in a Catholic monastery. The nuns took good care of him while his mother was struggling to survive in Theresienstadt during 1943.

She was fortunate enough to work in the kitchen until they shipped her to Wulkow in the autumn of 1944, a work camp near Berlin that was under the immediate command of Adolf Eichmann. She experienced terrible things there. One cold November day, the SS commander Stuschka locked her into a slit trench, completely naked. The guards would use these trenches that were dug into the ground and covered with wooden boards to protect themselves from grenade shrapnel. She squatted there for two days and nights. Her fingers froze. She barely survived, and since then her hands have never really been warm again.

At the beginning of 1945, she came back for a brief stay at an almost deserted Theresienstadt. She experienced the end of the war there and witnessed the utter misery of others from other concentration camps as the "city that the Führer had given to the Jews" was filled once again after the liberation – as a reception camp for the survivors arriving from other hellholes.

Immediately upon her return to Berlin, she was finally able to hold her son Peter in her arms again, and now here we were sitting in her room the evening before his birthday. I did not know what to say after she finished her story. I reached into my pocket and felt some provisions my mother had given me: a slice of bread smeared with liverwurst, one of her magic recipes made from roux, onions and marjoram, as well as something really special that was hard to find – a beautiful, big red apple. I handed Gertraud the sandwich and asked her to give the apple to Peter, my birthday present for him. Since that evening, we have been together – up until today.

After I had kept my head above water for several weeks by getting work in small bands playing in bars, getting potatoes from the Russians for my parents and major hangovers for myself playing in "middle-class" bars and going from table to table plucking Berlin songs, Viennese *schrammelmusik* (folk songs) and Hamburg songs – if requested, including *La Paloma* – I got a good gig in the *Greifi Bar* on Joachimsthaler Strasse.

The owner had hired the fiddle player Charlie Miller to lead a band. Charlie "Hot" Miller aka Karl Müller was a typical character of those times who dabbled in the black market. I was pretty innocent, so I was surprised when I was in the middle of a song and noticed that the drummer had unscrewed the bass drum and removed cigarettes by the carton: they were ten *reichsmarks* a piece! Since a carton went for two thousand marks, the value of the well-padded drum was huge on some evenings. Hot Miller dealt in brilliant-cut diamonds and whatever the market provided. These people made an amazing amount of money in a short time – unlike myself. I met with him and asked for advice after I had seen a guitar in a shop window on Rankestrasse that was haunting me in my sleep: a wonderful Roger for five thousand marks. Hot Miller just smiled, bought it and let me use it for my performances at the *Greifi*. I was slowly getting back on my feet again.

Then one day, somebody knocked on our door. It was Helmut Zacharias. He had just gotten back from captivity. We greeted each other with much affection. Right away, he asked if I would like to join a band he was putting together as he intended to play swing and jazz again. He did not yet have an offer to play anywhere, but he thought he had a good chance to resume his previous successful career. He invited Miller's Roger guitar and me to his apartment on Hohenzollerndamm the next day and put the sheet music for a pretty tough

**Helmut Zacharias (violin), Hans Nowak (bass) and Coco Schumann (guitar)
in the *Friedrichstadt-Palast*, Berlin, 1946**

guitar piece onto the edge of his bed and said, "If you can play this you've got yourself a job."

It was *Holiday for Strings*, and I liked it from the very beginning. I played well, he agreed, and he overcame my remaining reservations. I was making good money at *Greifi*, the tips were good, and I planned to stay there for now. But I agreed. There was a problem with the guitar, though. Helmut's fabulous wife Hella came up with a solution. She sold off her family jewels, met with Hot Miller, paid him the five thousand marks and bought the Roger for me. Later I paid her back little by little in installments from my fees. Tough yet very stimulating times lay ahead.

The Berliner Rundfunk (Berlin Radio Network) and later the Sender Freies Berlin SFB (Free Berlin Broadcasting) were administered by the Russians back then, and they organized tours for many German musicians. They drove us around the Soviet occupation zone in an open truck, and we were particularly happy to get a bus when the weather turned bad. We were a colorful group that included people like Hermann Held and Brigitte Mira.

We got into the truck at the studio on Masurenallee and drove off towards Neuruppin. On the way we stopped at a small town inn that was teeming with buzzed Russians. We could not decline an "invitation" to have a little drink with them. The complicating factor was that the drinks were made from some tainted alcohol, a terrible concoction called *alkolat* that could leave you blind; nobody remembered what it was made of. Hermann Held – whose motto was "Hermann Held (keeps) what he promises" – made the fatal mistake of trying to avoid the disaster by showing them a few card tricks. The result was that he alone was singled out for a bout of drinking. Water glasses were filled to the brim. He finally could not drink another single drop. Drawing his pistol, one of the Russians politely convinced him that it would be better if he kept on drinking . . . I have never seen a man this drunk; there was no way he could play that night! We had a lot of fun with the Russians even though it was not without its dangers. We had to be careful.

We played a club for an event hosted by a newspaper that was run by the Russians' *Neues Deutschland* (New Germany). Two soldiers requested different songs; one of them wanted a tango, the other a polka. The situation quickly spiraled out of control. There was shouting and yelling, we did not quite know what to do. We could not tell who was higher rank. Finally, one of them made it clear. He drew his pistol, stepped up to the stage, pointed at me, and his deep bass voice determined the unfolding of the remainder of the evening: "Polka!"

The fees from the Russians were generous and nutritional. Each of us got the courtesy bottle of vodka and several huge sacks of potatoes. We had to hand over a couple of sacks to some Russians when we went through a checkpoint, sure, but it was still a sensational haul. There was not much money around, however. Sometimes I did not even have the nickel I needed to take the trolley to Masurenallee, so I trudged all across the dusty town with my guitar.

The first jobs with the Americans at the Tempelhof Officer's Club changed everything. Each of us was paid with a carton of cigarettes. This was phenomenal. I could barter it for whatever I wanted. From here on, everything went better for me. Helmut's swing compositions and our arrangements were well received. Even the Americans and the British accepted them as original, new innovations of German jazz. They also could sense our preference for American-style songs.

Unfortunately, I do not remember too much about one special event; it almost got lost in the variety of experiences and events of those days. Marlene Dietrich had returned to her hometown of Berlin for a few days in September of 1945. A few pictures of her arrival at Tempelhof and her wearing an American officer's uniform, carrying her famous "singing saw" under her arm, appeared in the papers. She was going to entertain the troops in southern Germany and France when she heard that her mother was living in Berlin. A spectacular

reunion was arranged that did not find much resonance with the German people. Their great Marlene had become a *persona non grata*, a traitor to her country. The ongoing outrage was a deeply distressing indicator of the mood in the bombed-out country.

Even when her mother Josephine von Losch died two months later, the presence of the stars who had arrived for the funeral received only scant notice in the press. In early 1946, she gave a concert for the American Special Service at the *Titania Palast* that was not noticed much. Only her old friend, the actor Hubert "Hupsi" von Meyerinck knew about it because Rolf Italiaander had organized the show, *Swell Fair*, as well as the participating musicians, myself among them.

The atmosphere in the auditorium was charged and enthusiastic; the soldiers adored their Marlene no less than the rest of America. She did not have

Coco Schumann, 1946

this effect on me yet because I was not interested in the movie *Der Blaue Engel* (The Blue Angel), which came out before she left in 1934, and I did not have the opportunity to follow her career after that. When she went out on stage I immediately understood the reason for her reputation. With her head held high, she stepped out in her short uniform skirt and walked toward the edge of the stage, putting one of her famous legs in front of the other; a hush fell over the crowd, then she sang those Friedrich Hollaender songs she had taken from this city to the United States, that had provided the foundation for her world fame. She had given this song her best any number of times, at magnificent parties in Hollywood and at mud-covered American positions under fire from German tanks, in glittering ballrooms and stinking sickbays, but that evening in her home town was anything but routine. Even Dietrich in all her apparent perfection could not hide her feelings.

The people of Berlin did not read much about the sensational performance, and in any case, they were not interested. The *Melody-Illustrierte* (The Illustrated Melody) was the only publication to carry a story about the concert and my participation, and that was months later. The magazine was published by composer Gert Froboess, father of Conny, the singer who would soon exhort the nation to pack up their swimming trunks (in the monster hit *Pack die Badenhose ein*) . . .

The musical landscape changed once again. I had to reorient myself and began to see new perspectives in my own style. Popular music developed contemporary forms of entertainment and set itself somewhat apart from pre-war music. The death of Paul Lincke in September 1946 marked the end of an era in Berlin music history.

It was a bumpy ride for a while, but it was worth it. I escaped into my music and did not have any time, or did not want to have any time, to give in to hate or bitterness. The International Court in Nuremberg pronounced the verdict on twenty-two of the primary war criminals on October 1, 1946, following the trial of the main defendants of the Third Reich, and sentenced twelve of them to "death by hanging". I cannot remember my feelings when I heard this sentence. There were no real feelings of satisfaction. Anyone who has ever personally taken part in or suffered during a presumably "great historical event" knows that it was entirely different when it happened. Behind the greatest story, greatest joy or horror there is the small, mundane everyday routine. History takes place in books; other than that, life is just life, with reconciliation, denial and forgetting. Even I have had my successful little escapes.

We were in much demand at the radio stations. The later RIAS – still called DIAS back then, the wired radio in the American sector – was also broadcasting from mobile vans; their recording studios were inside a factory building at the Schmargendorf train station. I met lots of old acquaintances there and played with Fred Oldörp who was leading the Drei Travellers (Three Travelers). They had a real hit with his song *Ich hab noch einen Koffer in Berlin* (I Still Have a Suitcase in Berlin) with Fritz Schulze, who later called himself Schulz-Reichel and switched to comedy skits playing characters like "The off-tune piano player" and "Schräger Otto", and with the great clarinet player Detlef Lais, a student of Ernst Höllerhagen. The musicians changed bands quite often, from recording to recording. Helmut and I were the only ones who stuck together, whether we played as Helmut Zacharias und seine Solisten (Helmut Zacharias and his soloists) or the quickly famous Helmut Zacharias Quartet. We played any number of classics like Gershwin's *Liza, Lady Be Good* and *I Got Rhythm,* but mostly we played Helmut's own tunes such as *Lucky Strike* and *Swing 46.* I also contributed with my first composition, *Stoplight,* but Helmut took credit because I was not a member of the *Gesellschaft für musikalische Aufführungs -und mechanische Vervielfältigungsrechte* (GEMA) (Society for musical performing and mechanical reproduction rights).

I used to listen to one of my greatest idols, the American guitarist Charlie Christian, on the radio. He created a new sound that was unheard of and which made me curious at first, then quickly fascinated me. I met Roger Rossmeisel in the summer of 1946. His father, the famous guitar maker Wenzel Rossmeisel, had named his famous instruments after him. I took the opportunity to ask him about this amazing new sound. He knew all about it and told me about pickups, amplifiers and the ability to electrically modify the sound of the strings.

Since he was already familiar with these things that were Greek to me, he asked me straightaway if he should make one for me. Even though I had butterflies in my stomach, I handed over my beloved guitar, one he was entirely familiar with. There was plenty of material lying around to tinker with in those days. He took an old set of army headphones, took out the magnets, poured stearin in a small tin box and put the magnets inside – a genuine modern instrument. The bass player for Helmut Zacharias, Eugen Petrovich, a Bulgarian electrician, built me an amplifier using odds and ends left over from the war. When it would start to squeak too much, I would give it a slight tutorial kick. As far as I know I was the first musician in Germany to play on stage with an electric guitar. It was an absolute success, and my new sound did not conflict with Helmut's music, quite the opposite. The audience was thrilled by this new sound, the harbinger of a new, more carefree world.

We became more successful. After a live broadcast we would receive a mountain of fan mail. The pay was not that great but the excitement made up for it. After all, we did get our "hard" currency – cigarettes.

We were engaged to play for the English revue *Streamline Express* in the fall of 1946. We lived in Winsen an der Luhe with the other artists who were working for the Brits and drove from there in buses to various airports and barracks.

The fact that we didn't have any problems with the occupation forces was evidenced in that our employers kept changing. Right after we finished the *Streamline Express,* we were engaged by the Americans to play the Riessersee Hotel just outside Garmisch-Partenkirchen, not far from Wolfratshausen,

Coco with guitar, 1946

the place where I had regained my freedom. The hotel right next the famous Zugspitze mountain was a spa for overworked GI's. We all got to spend a real winter holiday with them.

The kicker was that we got to stay at the hotel itself, the only Germans who were allowed access. Someone had picked us at an audition in Heidelberg and apparently thought we were particularly good. We got full service, officer's mess and so-called PX-rations of cigarettes and sausages, the *class A* food coupons for those who did hard physical labor. Other bands got cards for *class B* coupons for difficult labor; the rest only got *class C* for "normal" work. We played like heavy laborers and did live broadcasts from the hotel for the AFN every Saturday. Down in Garmisch, Maxl Greger played the *Hotel zur Post* where it was not as comfortable . . . After all, people were starving and winter was harsh.

These days in the mountains were the first relaxation after these past years, the first tangible dream of living a good life. I felt good. Looking back, I think the privileged treatment was a kind of compensation for the tough years I'd had. The Americans probably knew about this. After Christmas, I took heart and asked if Gertraud could join me. They sent her a "travel order" right away, a document issued by the military. She dropped Peter off at his aunt's and came on an Allied forces train. We spent an unbelievably beautiful New Year's Eve together. Gertraud and I – some time before our wedding – even got to use, for the first time, an appropriate king-size bed.

Riders in the Sky

O N WHIT SUNDAY of 1947, after playing all night at a wild party, our gang was booked to play a matinee performance at the *Puhlmann* theater on the east side of town. We played one of the first numbers before the intermission. After breakfast, we went over to the Berlin broadcasting studios where we tootled live on air for an hour starting at four o'clock for teatime and dancing. This was followed by an hour-long break during which we took nourishment in liquid form before reporting to a General's party at eight o'clock at the *Harnack Haus* in Zehlendorf to stir things up. After a few rounds of that, an enormous American car pulled up with a liveried chauffeur at the wheel who drove us to a night performance at some club in Wedding. The chauffeur waited dutifully in the car while we were inside blasting away and took us straight back to the General's party where we played until five in the morning. I do not remember how I got home! And it was quite a typical day for us, so this made it almost mandatory for me to live with my parents, who took care of the many everyday issues.

By the spring of 1947, a small modification was imminent. Our band, with Rudi Bohn at the piano, Eugen Henkel on saxophone and Hans Nowak on bass, was booked for an entire season, from May to October, at the infamous *Al Sibarita Bar*, a pavilion with a view of the Baltic Sea over the beach at Timmendorf. Later on, this became the location of the legendary *Kuddel Daddeldu*. If you go there today all you see is a concrete base; next to it the enormous Maritim Hotel looms.

Even in those days, Timmendorf was a playground for music lovers and the newly wealthy, for everyone who could still, or yet again, afford to celebrate the new times with zing and without inhibition. For us, it was a truly exquisite job where we rarely saw daylight. We got up in the afternoon and had breakfast, rehearsed and started playing at nine or ten o'clock at night – until six in the morning, sometimes until eight. We sat on the beach for a while and let the breeze blow away our hangovers before disappearing in our beds.

Hella and Helmut Zacharias began to play a still greater role in my life. Hella took good care of us; we could always go to her with all of our problems and crises. She took especially good care of me. I needed someone like her since the *Al Sibarita* became both my place of work and my home, although I was never very clear about where all this was headed. It was a fairly opulent living room with countless plush chairs, an extraordinarily cool and fashionable interior decor and a bar that offered only the best. Accordingly, the customers ranged from Hamburg's black market operators to the industrialists of Germany's "first hour".

One of the most sought-after guests who frequented the Timmendorf bars was named Waldmann, a real character who was already making steel again and who threw money around like it was going out of style. A large silver plate in his head was hiding a wound he had gotten during the war. When he and his wife, a massive, bawdy Valkyrie, were on a roll the club owners would get on the phone and warn each other. The two of them would storm into a club, he would go up to the stage right away and hand out fantastic tips. If he was drunk, then he would fall down in front of the stage and toss bills all over the dance floor. He then usually went to the bar and sent the bartender away, declaring he was done for the evening. He took over the bar, handled the bottles and cocktail shakers and mixed one exceptional round after another for the whole club – according to color. First, the drinks were violet, then green and yellow . . . We kept having to drink them in one go, which may have been the best way to do it!

After tours like this we were in an excellent mood, and Rudi Bohn would take a header into the Baltic Sea, his accordion still strapped on. Waldmann's wife had fallen head over heels in love with Helmut and pulled out all the stops to have him for herself. I can still see how one morning he ran from the stage out the door with her hot on his heels, chasing him through a nearby forest – an unforgettable image – but she did not get him.

In those days we played the so-called Hoffmeister tours in the British and American zone several times, organized by the Hoffmeister agency in Mannheim. We got into some adventurous situations when we tried to slip through the Russian zone on army trucks, wearing British uniforms, without transit papers. The Russians had an agreement with the military, but they did not allow civilians to cross their zone just like that. The four powers did not get along *that* well to be swapping the best performers. We were smuggled like whisky during the prohibition. Hella Zacharias was with us, and she even brought along her three-year-old daughter Sylvia, who was hidden under a blanket while her mom had to hold her hand over her daughter's mouth when they passed through the Soviet checkpoint.

A colorful mix of artists got together on these tours. Werner Veidt, Iska Geri and Theo Lingen performed sketches; Gert Fröbe, thin as a rail, appeared as the *Frau von Gestern* (the "Woman from Yesterday") and recited Erich Kästner and Christian Morgernstern. Camilla Horn gave her best; Rudi Bohn presented *The Flight of the Bumblebee*; Lingen sang chansons; Lale Andersen performed various acts, while Gert performed "*alles Mögliche und Unmögliche*" (Everything Possible and Impossible). In between acts, Helmut Zacharias entertained with his soloists: Rudi Bohn on piano, Klaus Dillmann on bass, Kurt Grabert on drums and vibraphone, and me. The program proclaimed "two hours of the best fun" and "masterful evenings of entertainment". We tried hard to fulfill these promises.

The funniest place was backstage. We got along nicely with Gert Fröbe, who happened to be a good musician, a trained violinist. With the talented Theo Lingen I developed a curious, quiet friendship. He was extremely intelligent, dead serious and reserved, like all good comedians. He kept his distance from all the mayhem we caused. Even if we made a stop on our bus trips he did not join us inside the café. He was afraid people would start cracking up the moment they saw him. While we sat around and refreshed ourselves he went ahead, walking down the road all by himself and not bothered one bit. Later we would pick him up and give him something to eat and drink.

After we had been on stage together a few times, we got to know each other a little without saying much. He called me "Herr Jakobi", and I still do not know why. In Bad Pyrmont he knocked on the door to my hotel room and said: "Herr Jakobi, I would like to ask you to have a cup of coffee, my wife is visiting me." His wife was an opera soprano – and a Jew. It was a marvelous afternoon. He never said the reason for the invitation, but I think he knew my story. Over time, he used a couple of my jokes, something that made me incredibly proud. I comforted him the evening his daughter Uschi made her first appearance in Berlin – at the mere thought of it, he was suffering such a bout of stage fright he could hardly perform.

Ever since I began to earn some money, I had started wearing really cool ringlet socks from America. Theo Lingen asked: "Where did you get those strange socks? Oh, from America . . . terrible, terrible!" Later he was standing at the edge of the stage in front of the rampaging audience and sang his hit song *Theodor im Fussballtor* (Theodor the Goalie). In the middle of the song, he suddenly turned to me, grinned and pulled up his right trouser – striped socks!

The Hoffmeister tours and our engagement at Timmendorfer Strand often took us to Hamburg, where we had a certain following. We thought the city was attractive so we did not hesitate for long when the *Nordwestdeutsche Rundfunk* (Northwest German Broadcasting Network) offered the Helmut Zacharias Quartet a contract beginning in September of 1948. We moved to Hamburg in August.

The radio work provided us with our first regular income, and Hella Zacharias once again took care of all the rest. She even worked out rebates at the grocery stores when money was tight. We had to perform eight shows a month – some of them were four hours long – and additional songs as well. It was work, but it animated me to make a long-held wish come true.

As much as I liked Helmut, I sometimes envied him in a friendly sort of way that he – back when he was a wunderkind – had a solid musical education and I did not. I wanted to find out if an education would spur me on, and in October of 1948, I signed up at the *Konservatorium der Musik* (Conservatory of Music) at Klein-Flottbek for classes in guitar and theory of harmony with Fräulein Züchtig ("Mrs. Prudish"), whose name did honor to her.

I learned a lot there, but not for long. The courses were much shorter than today, and I received a classic concert education in a relatively short time. I was right; I had lacked the education I received. My instrument suddenly acquired new dimensions for me. Nevertheless, I did not want to stay with classical music. My music had its roots more in the long hours I had spent sitting on the wall at the *Delphi,* in the forbidden notes emanating from the exhaust ventilators, in the much too brief time spent with Hans Korseck and in the smoke-filled, beautiful hours of the various "first times". The feeling, this indefinable something had made me who I am. This could be aided only so much by an education. It must grow constantly from within – which is still true today.

By mid-March of 1949, shortly after Joe Louis retired from boxing after defending his heavyweight title for twelve years, I returned to Berlin after I had gotten out of my Hamburg contract and made Gertraud very happy, along with my parents and my little brother Jürgen, who had turned seven in the meantime. I got along great with my brother, and our relationship has lasted right up through today. But the age difference of eighteen years had a strong influence. We never played together like brothers. We were very happy every time we saw each other – which unfortunately was not all that often in those days.

The months that followed were topsy-turvy. I played on all the stages of the city, and that was not a small number. Hundreds of musicians were busy at the

An improvised café (bottom right) in a bombed out building on Kurfürstendamm (Charlottenburg),
as seen from Breitscheidplatz, August 8, 1949.
The *Ciro Bar* on Rankestrasse was located a few blocks away.

PHOTO: WILLY KIEL, F REP. 290 NO. 0002607 COURTESY: LANDESARCHIV, BERLIN

Kurfürstendamm and Zoo districts alone, musicians who were playing their broken hearts out. The mountains of rubble had not yet been removed, a lot of people still struggled, but at night the air was sizzling.

One of the most elegant clubs in Berlin was the *Ciro Bar* on Rankestrasse. Fritze Brandenburg, the owner, had been a headwaiter and a gigolo. He had hauled sacks of money out of open safes and vaults at the end of the war, had "collected" carpets and paintings and made a nice stash after the Zero Hour, which he invested in the breathtaking furnishing of his bar. As though it were common – just as it happened with Waldmann at the *Al Sibarita Bar* – a regular customer frequented the place, sending the bartender to the penalty box and conjuring up memorable cocktail rounds for the other customers. It was Curd Jürgens the movie star, in action.

I played at least eight hours almost every day, working just like a miner in the Ruhr district: going down into the mine at night and coming back in the morning at five. Mostly I did not make it home because I was so wired after playing it was pointless. We met in dark clubs to jam for hours with other musicians, traffickers, prostitutes, pimps and gamblers. Many of us immediately reinvested our earnings at playing roulette or cards, the only distraction I had always avoided. My parents were too poor, and I was way too close to them to risk losing the money we all needed. I was the bank for the band, so I did have a role to play in this enterprise. Colleagues came almost every evening to borrow money to tide them over until the next payday.

At the beginning of 1950, I finally felt secure and accepted in my profession. Critics praised my playing, and that did not hurt. An influential music magazine called *Viervierteltakt* (Four-four Time) regularly published a jazz poll of the best musicians in Germany. I was named best jazz guitar player several times in a row.

I tried to start my own band in Berlin. Helmut Zacharias was in Hamburg, and his success was phenomenal. He played a club called *Erholung* (Repose) with his sextet and with varying lineups. We took a break from each other, which did not put the slightest dent in our friendship. One of the first appearances of my new band was a spectacular jam session at the *Club Femina* on Nürnberger Strasse. We played a program that lasted for seven hours, with soloists from the Freddy Brocksieper Star Quintet, the Mischka Combo, the Rediske Quartet, the Joe Glaser Boptet and others. Among all the illustrious names on the poster there was the "Coco Schumann Combo". I took a certain amount of pride in that.

It was the time of the "band competitions" whose motto was *swing heil*, a reference to the relief we felt about regaining our new and old freedom. Dance music groups competed in all-nighters, playing foxtrot, boogie, swing and anything that was fashionable. A month later we were booked, together with the new, fast-rising Botho Lucas Trio and, to my personal satisfaction, the old Lubo D'Orio dance orchestra, who had fronted for us at the *Uhland Eck* club in 1941 while I was taking my first baby steps as a musician. Many of the former jazz and swing musicians had switched over to play popular music. This was not a problem for us in those days. We did not make distinctions but played anything. My combo played classics like *What Is This Thing Called Love, Body and Soul*, and *Lester Leaps In*, while our friends sang the songs of the top forty: *Kleiner Boy aus Porta* (Small Boy from Porta), *Ich muss mich mal wieder verlieben* (I Have to Fall in Love again), *Geisterreiter* (Ghost Rider) and Ilja Glusgal's *Der Ich-Du-Er-Sie-Eskimo* (a word play on pronouns).

The definitive tendency of the new German pop lyrics was rather apparent: it was time to be silly and sing with a throaty sound till you dropped, but it was only natural, five years after the end of the catastrophe and in the midst of numerous promises of the recovery. I did not have any problems with that, even though we preferred to stay close to our roots.

In the spring of 1950, Gertraud and I finally decided to move in together. We were very much in love. Her son Peter was living with us like he was my own child.

Coco Schumann with Helmut Zacharias (violin) and Manfred Hausknecht (drums), circa 1948

Coco Schumann and Botho Lucas, circa late 1940s

We had become a normal family even though our own unique fate had brought us together. Gertraud and I were kindred spirits. Even if we could not forget our individual fate, together we could deal with it due to similar basic experiences. It wasn't our painful memories that added up, it was the sheer joy we felt for having survived, for ourselves and for the other. Every day reminded us of the past: spiritually, emotionally, but also physically. Neither of us would ever be free from that. Our joy in life, the humor and our understanding for each other were strong enough. There was also a shared wariness, a certain mistrust, and we kept an eye on our unpredictable country. A small suitcase was always packed and standing ready in case we should need it, both in our minds and in our closet.

Despite the success I had had the previous months – we played the *Friedrichstadt-Palast* along with Kurt Abraham, Ferry Juza, Ilja Glusgal, Werner Neumann and others, alongside Cuban dance scenes, film step dancing attractions and Ilse Hübener's vocal solo in a revue called *Aus der Luft gegriffen* (Out of Thin Air) – I was feeling a strange uneasiness. Perhaps some things need a little time before they manifest themselves. I could not forget the endless days in the camps. I could not forget the images, my grandparents, the children, my friends, Fricek . . . I did not *want* to forget them anymore. Slowly I realized what had happened to us, to my family, during those years. With hindsight I was able to overcome my feelings of shame. Four years earlier, I had been convinced that my country, Germany, had left behind that evil era for good, that the murderers and their accomplices had been punished, but now even I finally realized this belief was an illusion, despite the good spirits around me – that it was wishful thinking and an illusion. The reports began to add up, in small ways and large, that way too many people remained inconvincible and that German nationalism with all its lethal implications had not been conquered.

Lots of people who had survived the death camps felt threatened that year. In January, the first cases of "former" Nazis emerged in the press who had purchased their get-out-of-jail-free cards for a certain amount of money. By August 1950, the first prisoners sentenced at the Nuremberg Trials were released due to "good behavior". The dangerous tendency of our countrymen was not easy to get a grip on. It was not clear to us whether anyone was even trying to do so. Politicians argued and debated ferociously – about rearmament.

Our doubts about Germany grew and finally gained the upper hand. For a short time we asked ourselves whether Israel would be an alternative; in the meantime, even Great Britain had officially recognized it. My bond with the

Jewish faith, however, was not that close; moreover, the situation there did not seem all that secure. We chose the United States. Uncle Arthur had found a home there and was happily engaged in the most curious endeavors.

We got busy getting ready for the trip. But our plans suffered a major setback. My mother had become a member of the SED, the *Sozialistische Einheitspartei Deutschlands* (Socialist Unity Party) – the governing party of Communist East Germany – because she felt it was the only political party that wanted to deal with the past. The American response was straightforward: her visa was denied, despite her suffering under the Nazi regime. For the first time, we experienced the new polarization of the world up close and personal, the fact that even in a democracy the individual did not count for much, something we considered to be a prerequisite for a lovable and democratic country.

We had to make a decision. Gertraud, Peter and I wanted to emigrate to Australia but my parents and my brother wanted to stay in Berlin. The uncertainty and the strain of a trip to this apparently adventurous continent was too much for them. Gertraud, on the other hand, was ready. Her career did not play a role as Dr. Fabian, the head of the *Institut für die Opfer des Faschismus* (Institute for the Victims of Fascism), the OdF, had left for the United States that spring.

We signed a contract with the Australian government which stipulated that the immigrants would pay for the trip to Australia and had to accept any work assigned to them for a period of two years. It was not a simple step to take. We took it because of the need we felt to leave, not entirely voluntarily, but we were confident and excited at the thought of the new world and the uncertainty that lay before us. We were young, we stuck together and, after all, what could go wrong?

While we were getting ready to leave, I signed a contract with the Roger guitar company. I wanted to be their representative in Australia and eventually develop a distribution network over there. I got a guitar with a brilliant sound, the junior boss' masterpiece that he had built for his final exam as a guitar maker, an exam he passed with honors. Everything was set. At the beginning of October, Gertraud and I got married. We gave our notice of departure on October 16.

Farewell was harder than expected. Right up until the moment we left, my friends and colleagues were asking me if I knew what I was doing. Even Helmut tried to talk me out of it and declared me to be crazy to be leaving my home country at the peak of my career. However, our decision to try to escape the past was firm. It was hard to explain because they would have understood only if we had told them everything that had happened. We could not and did not want to do that.

On the Sunny Side
of the Street

THE FIRST STAGE of the adventure already started in the East Frisian town of Aurich, where a transit camp for emigrants had been set up. The first evening in the camp – how could it have been otherwise? – I met a friend, the Berlin accordionist Bernhard Schneidewind. We played an emotional and strange farewell concert for our country. From Aurich, we made our way to Cuxhaven. Finally, my wife, her son and I stood on the deck of the *Castelbianco* and left our difficult homeland behind. Endless expanses lay before us, a voyage of six weeks to the end of the world. We were sailing on a "floating death trap", a narrow Italian troop transport that swayed so much even during calm seas that all of the passengers were hanging over the rails and fed the fishes with the modest meals served to them on the ship. My beloved Gertraud was the only one who sat there in the morning as chipper as can be at the breakfast table, wondering what the fuss was all about.

During the voyage, we had diligently worked on our English; when we finally arrived in Melbourne we felt ready for the unknown country. I could already see that it had not been a mistake to come here when I took my first steps onto Australian soil. This country was receiving us warmly, a sign hung over a registration control counter, one that would never have been behind a government counter in Germany: "Please remember: we are here for you, not you for us." We were in a democratic country!

First we were shipped to Bonegilla, to a former army camp where immigrants from all over the world were waiting for their turn. The officials from the Immigration Department were not easy to get along with. They played an incomprehensible game when distributing the jobs. A bricklayer or a writer would be assigned to work at an orchard. A farmer had to deal with a

On the ship *Castelbianco* to Australia with my wife Gertraud and Günther Breitkreuz, 1950

construction job. Anybody who turned down their assignment would be sent back to their country of origin and had to pay for both fares and possibly even a fine for breach of contract. I was uneasy with the thought of hurting my hands picking fruit, but I reminded myself that life had been full of surprises so far. I was right about that. We had barely settled in at Bonegilla when I decided to have a look at the classified pages of an Australian paper, where musicians from all over the world were looking for a job, when somebody called out my name and gave me a warm greeting. I did not know how to place him, but the important thing was that he knew me.

He led me through the camp and introduced me to a number of musicians. Germans, Hungarians, Czechs and Poles, a strange mix of people had assembled here. Some of them knew my name and my music, either from the radio or from the winner lists of the jazz polls. Joschi, a Hungarian pianist, asked me straight away if I wanted to play in the camp band – silly question! I was back on a bandstand my first night in camp, back on the stage that meant the world to me.

My worries were not over, though. Later on, an opportunity popped up that just begged to be taken advantage of. The capital of Australia, Canberra, was celebrating a *Commonwealth Jubilee,* and the newly-arrived musicians from Bonegilla were invited to play. Ballet, music of every kind, a buffet stretching out for a mile or two was set up on well-groomed lawns hosting the most select guests Australia had to offer. Typically Australian: we stood around outdoors in the freezing night, drinking enormous amounts of beer despite the prohibition. During the breaks we were watching the spectacle, rather awestruck, when Joschi gave me a nudge: "Well, lookie there. Do you know who that is? It's Armstrong, the Minister of Labor."

I put my plate down, took my heart in hand, buttoned my jacket and marched straight up to him. He turned to me, and I peppered him with my clubhouse English: "Excuse me, Sir! My name is Coco Schumann. I came from Berlin a few days ago, and I'm a musician. Music is my life, and I am not able to live as a fruit picker in a little village without the possibility of playing my guitar." Mr. Armstrong stared at me, somewhat bewildered, but seemed more amused than upset by my imposition. I then asked him if he would be able to see to it that we were assigned to a somewhat larger city. He grinned and asked one of his people to take down my name, telling me I should call him when my name came up.

A short time later, I was called to the employment office where I was told that I had been assigned to pick fruit in some small town. I said: "Excuse me, but you need to call Mr. Armstrong. He's going to give you different instructions." The official looked at me like I had three noses. He started to rant and rave, but I was stubborn. He got on the phone – what a country! – and briefly spoke with the department. I saw his face fall to the floor. "It's all right. He goes to Melbourne."

This is how we came to the big city. We found a beautiful apartment despite the shortage by way of a tip from Fredel Neufeld, a shoemaker who knew Gertraud from the concentration camps and who had already settled down in Melbourne. We were happy. However, I had to work at an Australian jam factory and unload heavy tubs of sugar into marmalade pots. After two weeks, my hands looked like they shouldn't even get close to a halfway decent guitar. If I wanted to continue playing guitar, I had to do something. I inquired about the possibilities my new hometown had to offer.

Then I loaded my heavy amplifier onto my back using furniture-packing straps, took my new Roger guitar and trudged down the street to St. Kilda Beach, a posh beach area of Melbourne. That's where *The Oran Coffee Lounge* was located, the most exclusive address in town. The man who watched me arrive was appalled when he saw me climb up the steep stairs with my amplifier strapped to my back. It turned out he was the owner. I explained to him that I was from Berlin and had not played in a long time. I told him I just wanted to join in. He asked his musicians, who rolled their eyes – a petulant virtuoso from

Berlin, the last thing they needed. But they let me give it a try and asked which key I wanted to play in. When I said I did not care, they were highly amused about this strange little pretender in their midst.

So anyway, after the first tune I got a coffee that hid the whisky in it – alcohol was prohibited after six in the afternoon – and I was in. Then the kitchen door flung open and someone came in who could not believe what he saw. Walter Jockel from Theresienstadt, the butcher from the camp kitchen.

Walter Jockel had been a fan of mine. In front of him was the young, sweet – and naive – boy who had enchanted everyday life in Theresienstadt with his guitar playing. He had returned to me the haunch of beef, which was the payment for a private room, without any words. Now he was the manager of *The Oran Coffee Lounge* and immediately asked me if I wanted to continue to play that very same evening. The audience consisted of an international mix of people from all sorts of countries: Poles, Hungarians, Americans, Greek, Russians and so on – a hodgepodge that was right up my alley. The biggest success I had that evening was with a couple of Romanian tunes that brought the house down.

It had worked out once again. As I was leaving the owner said, "Leave the guitar here and come back on Friday." I explained to him I was under contract and had to stir marmalade. He promised he would call the employment office first thing in the morning and request me for a gastronomy job. It worked. The remainder of my two-year work contract was spent toiling away night after night – as a kitchen helper wearing a tuxedo on stage.

Gertraud and Peter were also getting along fine. Australia was a wonderful country, a dream come true. Parrots were flying through the air, we lay under palm trees and ate huge golden peaches – everything else was immeasurably far away. Whenever we talked with Walter about Theresienstadt everything seemed even more unbelievable, in the midst of this new world, in Melbourne, Victoria, at 39 Union Street, West Preston.

After two years of playing *The Oran Coffee Lounge,* there were numerous new contacts for the "free" time later on. I let the general representative contract with Roger expire since I would have had to travel up and down the enormous country at the expense of my music. Instead, I tried my luck at the clubs and bars of Melbourne, Sydney and Canberra.

One evening an elderly gentleman who had come to listen to us at the club introduced himself. Heinz Gehl had played in Berlin before the war and had been a famous piano player even back then. I knew him only by name from those days and that he had played with William Mac Allen and Sydney Bechet.

At *The Oran Coffee Lounge* – St. Kilda Beach, Melbourne, Australia, 1953

He was one of those few who had read the sign of the times and emigrated to Israel, where he played at his brother's establishment, *The Atom Bar* in Tel Aviv. Like many other emigrants he soon left the promised land and returned to Melbourne. Now he was standing in front of me. My playing had intrigued him, and he offered me a session. He also asked to say hello to William Mac Allen when I returned to Berlin. A gesture like this from an old master was significant for a young grasshopper like me because contacts like this could lead to the next good job.

I also got to know Leo Rosner. He and his brother Harry, older by thirteen years and a violin player, had played in the concentration camps. We were connected by a quiet understanding; we did not talk much, but we played. Later I read that the Rosners had been saved by Oskar Schindler, who had requested they work at his factory and in doing so, got them to some sort of safety.

Singles by "Leo Rosner and his Gypsy Band" which featured my contributions began to appear at the record shops. We played rumba, Russian tangos and samba. The baritone Peter Kotek did the vocals. We often played at Jewish weddings and bar mitzvahs and traveled through half of Australia with a fashion show.

We had plenty of gigs and some of the new friends included "old acquaintances". I got to know André Schuster, the former bass player for Teddy Stauffer among many other European musicians. I had not forgotten his face and his playing. He enjoyed listening to my story about my box seat on the garden

With Bernhard Schneidewind in Melbourne, 1952

wall of the *Delphi.*

Not only for sentimental reasons did I want to return to jazz. *Downbeat,* a huge music festival, was held every year in Melbourne; it brought together the best Australian and international stars. I experienced the festival for the first time in 1952. The aura of those days inspired me to do arrangements and to give composition a try.

In September of 1953, the *Downbeat! Big Band Bash* was held once again at the round of Melbourne's Wirths' Olympia. Together with the best bands and special guest Liz Taylor we entered the competition with a version of "Jazz at the Phil Team" and, under the baton of Lowell Morris, whose hit song *North West Passage* I had played years ago in Berlin, we played the Australian interpretation of this legendary form of American jam session.

This is where I played *On the Sunny Side of the Street* for the first time with the tenor saxophone player Geoff Kitchen for his record *Melody Lingers.* At the same time, the album *Rhythm Cocktail* by the Coco Schumann Quintet appeared on the same label, Spotlight Varieties, which distinguished itself by the use of a new revolutionary recording technology, the microgroove technique (shellac albums would soon be obsolete), featuring among other numbers Irving Berlin's *Always,* Cole Porter's *What Is This Thing Called Love,* as well as two curious, charming arrangements by myself: Boccherini's *Minuet* and *Sur le pont d'Avignon.* The critics acclaimed both recordings, and they got a lot of play on the radio. In a relatively short time, I had gotten a good reputation in my new homeland.

I was not satisfied, though. Things were different in Australia. When we stepped out onto the street after we finished playing we encountered a ghostly silence. For us it was "high afternoon", the clock had (already) struck midnight, not a soul to be seen. *St. Kilda Junction*, a small milk bar frequented by taxi drivers was the only place open in all of Melbourne. I would hang out there for two or three hours and could only drink milkshakes . . . I could not take this for much longer. In Berlin at this time of night my friends would be moving on to the next club, and certainly not the last one!

I thought about my parents and brother a lot. They were far away, and I had many occasions to miss them. Deep inside I felt homesick – not for the fatherland as such but for a certain familiarity.

A letter from Günther Becker from Adelaide arrived, the former drummer for Walter Dobschinski. He was working for a railroad company and was planning to come to Melbourne. He stayed with us, of course, and we quickly got lost in conversations about the loud days in Berlin. He was not happy, here, either. When his visit came to an end, he announced: "Coco, I'm going back!" I answered: "Me, too!"

Once more, everyone thought I was insane. I had just laid the groundwork for having success with my music and bright prospects to earn good money, and I was going to walk away from it. There wasn't an alternative. The *Downbeat Festival* was held at the Exhibition Concert Hall on June 17, 1954. Once again the Coco Schumann Quintet performed with Stan Walker at the piano, Lou Silbereisen on bass, Lowell Morris on drums and Wally Wood on bongos and vocals. The newspapers trumpeted the farewell performance of "our first-rate group with top flight musicians" with quite a fanfare, which did not make leaving any easier. I did not want to do any long-range planning. I had learned not to . . . Today mattered, and perhaps tomorrow. I wanted to go back to Berlin whatever the cost. My mother had always said: "If you don't plan anything, nothing can go wrong!"

Saying goodbye to our Australian friends was painful. Leo Rosner and his Gypsies waved goodbye from the pier; they played our music when we went on board July 1. While I listened, I was not so sure I was doing the right thing anymore. We got to the railing, waved goodbye to our friends and began to look forward to the uncertain days ahead in our new, old homeland. Considering our financial situation, we took the *Toscana*, another Italian "coffin ship" that would sail its last voyage with us on board to Genoa where it would be decommissioned. We reached the high seas quickly, and there was no going back.

As though it was fate, I glanced at a bass player who was hurrying across the fore part of the deck with his huge bass fiddle case some time after we cast off. He was looking for his partner, a piano player. Both of them were excellent jazz musicians from Perth who were going to Italy to conquer Europe. We had a problem that first evening. They only had direct current on board the ship, and my amplifier could not use direct current. We talked to the ship's engineer into making a transformer for us, and as soon as it was ready, we started playing jazz for our fellow passengers.

During our layover in Colombo, the capital of Ceylon, we met the Hotel magnate Donovan Andrews. He invited us to join him for the evening and play at the best club in town. We had a big success there as well and enjoyed the evening thoroughly in the company of girls performing for the Paris-based Folies-Bergère. The voyage back was a terribly careening back and forth business, but it was really swinging, as well. Just before we arrived in Genoa, the two musicians decided to go to Berlin with me. I already had the basis for a new band.

Foolish Things

FOR ME, *"Heimat"* (homeland) is a sword that cuts both ways. I used to love it, but when I realized I could not forgive what Germany had done to me, I left. Being separated from my native country by a great distance, I missed it too much. When we set foot on German soil again, I immediately longed for the open, friendly everyday life I had enjoyed in the Australian democracy and became quite enraged by the narrow-minded German bureaucracy. At that moment, I knew that I did not have a home anywhere. I did want to return, but there was no Heimat for me anymore. Wherever I am, I do not fit in. Since I always see a glass as half-full rather than half-empty I can tell myself that wherever I am, I am in the right place, even without a homeland. I can live anywhere. Gertraud and I agreed not to buy any more expensive furniture and to keep that small suitcase packed and ready to go – at least in the back of our minds. It has been that way for all these years now, right up to today.

We had just arrived in Berlin when I ran into my jazz poll competitor, Johannes Rediske, while on a bus. We immediately agreed to play together. He was very happy about our return to Germany, and the news spread quickly. On August 24, 1954, we gave official notice to the authorities that we had returned.

Our two Australian friends thought Berlin was fascinating, so they decided to stay for some time. We had our first performance on September 18 in a show called " . . . *endlich wieder Jazz im Sportpalast*" (" . . . Finally – Jazz Returns to the *Sportpalast*") with Lubo D'Orio and Walter Dobschinski as well as the Trio Coco Schumann, Australia, which sounded rather exciting. Following a few performances broadcast from radio studios we performed a month later as the Coco Schumann Quintet as "guests from Melbourne" on a "big, colorful Sunday afternoon" at the Jahn Stadium, in a concert called *Au Warte!* (Oh My!) The date of the concert had been postponed "to give thousands of working people a chance to attend".

A few things had changed during our absence. I quickly noticed that it also had repercussions for my music. The radio stations were giving airtime almost exclusively to pop music. Even Bully Buhlan was churning out hits like *Ich hab dir aus Ägypten einen Kaktus mitgebracht* (I Brought You a Cactus from Egypt) and *Würstchen mit Salat* (Sausages with Salad). I had seen the first indications of this before leaving for Australia. Now I could see that a new age of music had dawned.

We played jazz, but a symptom began to develop in music that continued into the seventies until the renaissance of old-fashioned jazz. Jazz became more subjective and interiorized and was more or less secretly in the background of everything that the moods of those years brought forth. For most pop musicians, it was the soul and the essence of what they had to do in order to make a living from their profession, no matter the form they chose to play – slushy songs, carnival, folklore or "experimental" pop and rock variations.

The first shimmering silvery-blue glare of a new mass medium appeared on the horizon of the modern world and took shape – inside of strange teak and oak cabinets. Modern man did not listen to the radio anymore; he watched television. Slowly but surely it developed to become the dominant force in entertainment, bar none. I was quickly introduced to this new medium. In that first year back in Berlin, I played with various bands on a program called *3 x 3* and on *The Hit Parade*. I even appeared a few times with Helmut Zacharias who had made a name for himself with his "enchanted violin", and he was more popular than ever.

On the side, I tried to find solid engagements and in 1956 wound up with William Mac Allen's band that was playing *The Taboo Club*, owned by the Blatzheim Entertainment Group, by way of the greetings from Heinz Gehl I brought all the way from Australia. Blatzheim owned and managed an entertainment company that included several restaurants, clubs and other entertainment venues in all the larger cities of Germany. This company was operated according to strict standards. The musicians had to function like a supplier of goods. It was their personal business whether they could get some satisfaction from their job.

In Mac Allen's band we did not have any problem with that because our good mood was considerable, but the job required a decision that would point me in a new direction. Letters from my friends arrived from Australia. Leo Rosner wrote, "People are asking about you. You can start immediately. If you are really coming back, come back as quickly as you can." Spotlight Varieties had made an unsuccessful attempt to sell my records in Germany, but they continued to sell well in Australia and had good reviews. The prospect of an artistically independent jazz career overseas was tempting, but we stayed. The continuous back and forth between the two countries seemed weird even to me. The jet set in its modern day did not exist yet, otherwise I might have belonged to it, literally. My motive was less about the search for the latest event, it was about a deep sense of anxiety and uncertainty we felt about staying in one place, this place. That was not just the curiosity native to my passionate musician's soul; it was certainly the result of our very personal experiences in the Third Reich that had destroyed our basic trust in humanity – a prerequisite for any sense of home.

So the world had to come to me. The international stars were meeting in Berlin again in those days. It was self-evident that we musicians would seize the opportunity to hold jam sessions. As a jazz and swing player, I enjoyed the unbelievable advantage of having a home in my music and a family all over the world. I could not play with the jazz greats in Sydney, London, Las Vegas or New York, but I could play with all the great ones just outside of Berlin, in Charlottenburg. If the megastars were in town they usually did what we all did after a concert. The night was still young, and the hotel room was a desolate place. So they hopped from bar to bar and from club to club to see what their colleagues were up to. One of the best-kept secrets was a club called *Die Badewanne* (The Bathtub). Johannes Rediske was playing there, and I was often asked to join in with the band. That's where the jazz greats came to listen. When the spirit moved them they just climbed up on the bandstand and played with us. We met Dizzy Gillespie that way, an unbelievably nice guy and a real clown. Louis Armstrong, who once said to me during a break after a session when I mentioned my doubts about the prevailing trends in music: "Coco, it's not important what you play. It's important how you play it." He gave a demonstration of what he meant by playing an elegant, spontaneous version of *Es war einmal ein treuer Husar . . .* (Once There Was a Loyal Husar . . .). I thought about his words for many of the years that followed when we were in the musical doldrums in terms of marketplace entertainment.

In January of 1957, Heinz Dischereit, the owner of *Studio 22* on Leonhardstrasse, made me a tempting offer I could not refuse. He wanted me to start a band of my own at his establishment. I agreed and signed a contract with him as a "dance bandleader and musical artist", as I had to call myself to be able to get certain tax breaks. I set out to find a handful of fine musicians.

Dizzy Gillespie in Berlin, 1953

**Jam session with Lennie Niehaus, Bill Perkins, Manfred Burtslaf,
Stan Kenton (hidden), Coco Schumann, Hajo Lange and Mel Lewis**
Studio 22, Berlin, 1957

Ella Fitzgerald, Dizzy Gillespie, Ray Brown, Milt (Milton) Jackson and Timmie Rosenkrantz
Downbeat, New York City, circa September 1947
PHOTO BY WILLIAM P. GOTTLIEB, GOTTLIEB COLLECTION, LIBRARY OF CONGRESS

We had a good name in no time at all. The *Badewanne*, on the other hand, was considered somewhat out of style, which can easily happen to any club. Dischereit saw an opening and took it. He would drive his Rolls Royce out to the airport and offered the jazz greats a ride to their hotel that was worthy of their status. During the ride, he would ask the artists whether he could pick them up after their concert and show them some of the nightlife of Berlin. After the illustrious colleague finished his performance, he would be driven to *Studio 22* and could see for himself that we also knew what swing was all about. Sometimes some memorable combinations were playing on stage. I still have fond memories of an evening with the West Coast alto sax player Lennie Niehaus, with Bill Perkins and the New York drummer Mel Lewis. That was an exceptional session – a spectacular evening like many others that took place when members of our international family got together.

Then the moment arrived. I glanced up from my guitar and saw her sitting at one of the front tables. She was wearing a dress with a large floral pattern and was discreetly chic, with this drive within her and this wonderful laugh; everything about her evinced the incomparable artist – Ella Fitzgerald! She was rumored to never join in with other bands, but when we played *Foolish Things* she got up, grabbed the microphone and sang in a way that made our knees weak. I felt like I was thirteen again, hanging out at the Weba ice cream shop, sitting in front of the postal inspector's Lido briefcase, listening to her young voice. So much had happened in the intervening years, most of my pals from those days were buried somewhere – swing had survived, and I was part of it. Ella's chorus brought me back to the present. It was a grandiose night that would be repeated the next evening following her second concert. Those evenings at *Studio 22* with the large family of musicians on the bandstand – and Curd Jürgens serving drinks from behind the cocktail bar – were quite something.

I signed with Erwin Glomb's Le Nora Quintet the following spring. The engagement began at a club called the *Kupferkanne* (The Copper Pot) in Göttingen. Such changes of scenery were helpful if you made your living with music and wanted to provide for your family. We got along famously, and the new job offered a pleasant broad spectrum. Glomb valued my predilection for South American music, a style that was just beginning to catch on, and so we spent the nights playing sambas, mambo and cha cha cha together with not inconsiderable amounts of alcohol.

One evening, a guest whose face I knew from Berlin, came to greet me. He was producing the Heinz Erhardt feature film *Witwer mit fünf Töchtern* (The Widower and His Five Daughters) in Göttingen for the German motion picture studio Hansa. He spontaneously asked me if I would be interested in taking part. Vera Tschechowa and Susanne Cramer would also be in it. I accepted; to seal the deal we proceeded to drink each other under the table, so the makeup people had a hard time getting us fledgling rock and roll stars ready for the first take. We were only in one scene, but it was a lot of fun, and we really gave it our all. I loved the funny way that Erhardt confronted the deceitfulness and meanness of the world with innocent, hair-raising silliness. We got along well in private, too. He was much more pensive and deeper than his comedies would indicate. His audience did not understand a lot of his humor, as he wanted to show the Germans the new lies they were living with under the niceness and shallow harmony of the new *Wirtschaftswunder* (economic miracle).

Rock and roll slowly won the legs and hearts of teenagers eager to live life, but we were won over, too. We "older people" – after all, by 1958 I had counted a considerable thirty-four summers – were all for it, to compensate for the new "*Fresswelle*" ("wave of gluttony") that was sweeping Germany. Elvis Presley climbed to new heights of fame while he was stationed at the Hessian town of Friedberg and even climbed up the charts on the radio. At the end of

Film still from *Witwer mit fünf Töchtern*, 1957

Coco Schumann in the *Kupferkanne* in Göttingen with the band from *Witwer mit fünf Töchtern*, 1957

October, Bill Haley and the Comets were making scandals and got into fights in Hamburg and in Berlin at the *Sportpalast*. James Dean the rebel had died three years before and had become a legend. Traute (Gertraud) and I went to the concert at the *Sportpalast* and were swept away. But when Haley played his anthem *Rock around the Clock*, a few punks started hurling chairs and even a grand piano through the air and caused damages amounting to thirty thousand marks. We slipped away silently to avoid being among the eighteen arrested or the seventeen injured. The next morning, the newspapers were brimming over about the riot as if such a thing had never happened before. I read the outraged commentary to Traute, more amused than upset. Riots and rebels without a cause did not bother me much. The fuss that the mainstream media made about

Enrico, Margot Friedländer, Peter Rückert and Coco Schumann, 1958

the incident seemed inane and out of all proportion with the impact it might have on future political developments. It was merely a fear of change, even though back then change was the order of the day.

I earned my living mainly through radio and television appearances, alternating between Wolfgang Gabbe and his Soloists, the Berlin All Stars conducted by Dobschinski, Erwin Lehn and others, as well as my own combo, and in shows like the *Rediske Show, Rhythmus in Bildern* (Rhythm in Pictures) and *Musik am Montag* (Music on Monday). I did everything to stay in the business. Swing and improvisations were out, and the old German musical chestnuts did not interest me at all. I decided to compose Latin American dance music, which provided a large variety of styles. I really enjoyed this music and, besides, it provided the only possibility for you to improvise, to play freely, to add some jazz and to display whatever you wanted.

Following a program conference with Alfred Jack at the Sender Freies Berlin Radio, we were somewhat bored with the obligatory program selections. I took out a piece I had written, *Señorita de la Mambo,* and handed it to him. He liked it right away, and we recorded it. He gave me free rein for the next few months, and I did not even have to show anybody what I had composed before recording. Erich Hagenstein, a well-known lyricist, supplied the lyrics for my boleros, mambos and calypsos; they had airplay on the radio, were bought by sheet music publishers and they made their way up the charts – although not to the heights – however, they sometimes took a curious route. My name appeared on many different occasions, in different bands and now, playing my own compositions. Thus, the audience was in danger of becoming so confused they would not know who I was. I decided on an elegant solution: from one make two. Part of my show would be aired under the pretty Latin American pseudonym Sam Petraco, a name I made up using letters from Peter, Traute and Coco.

When I was back at the SFB studio to record a show, a Brazilian delegation buying German music dropped by. The gentlemen were surprised to hear a few bars of my music. They peered into the studio to see the Brazilian who was playing. They were astonished to see me. They snapped up all my compositions and took them to Brazil to play them on the radio over there. I felt like I had sold Coca-Cola to America.

Still, I was not able to become a real businessman. None of my songs ever became a hit; even my efforts to become the general representative of the Fender Guitar Company through contacts with Don Randle, the president, did not work out because in the final analysis I was a musician, not a salesman. This does not mean that a better coup can't follow on the heels of a failed coup . . .

I was one of the first musicians back then who owned a Gibson Les Paul with three pickups. The two Roger guitars I owned no longer suited my new style of playing. Our apartment was small and Traute kept tripping over the large cases and complaining, and rightfully so. When a man asked me about a Roger guitar following a concert I sold it to him, the first one. Later I also sold the second one, the one that was given to me to take to Australia. Each one was sold for two hundred and fifty marks – insane! If I had kept them and sold them today they would bring the equivalent of a trip around the world.

I played the Les Paul and could not have been happier with it. Then I needed an acoustic guitar for Gabbe's big band, which I could not afford. The head of a guitar company in Erlangen came to my rescue. He asked me to let him have the Les Paul for three days. In return, I could pick out a new Framus "Atilla Zoller", named after the famous guitar player. I got the instrument I desperately needed by way of this "industrial espionage", and I was satisfied, as opposed to my wife, who still had to do slalom between the instrument cases in the hallway and bedroom.

The nightlife was as turbulent as ever. Even though it seemed more tame and orderly than it was in the short time I spent in the clubs before I was arrested, the mood was animated by a carefree hope regarding the economy, miracles and modernism. After the afternoon tea dances we provided with Gabbe I would go home for my "lunch break" so I would make it through the second "shift" that started at nine or ten in the evening.

When we left our workplace at two or three in the morning, under the influence of light North German wines named "Doornkaat" ("Doormat") or "Linie" ("Stripe"), I was hauling my guitar case from club to club and usually wound up at the *Weisse Mohr* (White Moor) opposite the *Café Kranzler*. I would have some dinner while the sun came up. Once I ended up in the *Old Eden Bar* on Damaschkestrasse, and the piano player asked me to join in. He was a jazz fan who had appreciated my music for a long time. René Kollo and I played Erroll Garner's hit *Misty* and have frequently played together since then.

Touring was a strenuous affair, especially when we played the large dance halls in Wachtum near Löningen and a rock and roll party with the Hully Gully in the *Germanenclub* – at the "German Club", me of all people! We played slop, twist and boogie night after night and had to come up with something we liked for ourselves so we could endure the boredom week after week.

I believe such a lifestyle has to eventually be a problem for any live music performer. At home I had a family I lived with and loved, and "out there" I had a family I could not live without that often kept me much busier than my own family. It was certainly not easy for Gertraud. I am sure she secretly wished I had been a plumber many times, with evenings off and all the rest of the good stuff. In the end, she knew the way I was and supported my irregular lifestyle with forbearance and patience.

I loved her very much; after all, in 1961, she, Peter and my brother were all I had. My father had died in 1958, and my mother died two years later.

I did not adopt Peter, but he has always accepted me as a kind of father. He was studying law at that time, and since he was worried, with good reason, that he would not be able to pursue a career using his mom's family name, Goldschmidt, he asked me if he could officially change his name to Schumann. This was not a problem, even though the thought that it might be necessary was bitter.

Gertraud and Peter had to spend several weeks without me when I was on tour. I recently discovered a school notebook while cleaning up in our apartment where Gertraud had jotted down her thoughts. I found a poem she had written. It was a simple poem and expressed a tenderness that touched me. It was called "Longing".

Wochen sind's, seit ich dich sah	*It's been weeks since I've seen you*
Mir scheint's, es wären Jahre.	*It seems like it was years.*
Stunden dehnen endlos sich,	*Hours stretch out endlessly*
Minuten werden Tage.	*Minutes become days.*
Sehnsuchtsvoll erwart' ich dich	*I wait for you filled with longing*
zu jeder Tagesstunde	*At every hour of the day.*
Alles, was an Glück es gibt,	*Everything that fortune brings*
Ich träum's an deinem Munde.	*I dream it's on your lips.*
Komm zu mir – umarme mich	*Come to me – embrace me*
Und sprich von deiner Liebe.	*And tell me of your love.*
Ich bin dein; ich liebe dich,	*I am yours, I love you,*
wünsch', dass es stets so bliebe.	*Hope it will always be so.*

This is how it would be.

The special friendships that come up in show business provide a certain trade-off for the family life we give up when we go on the road. Some of them last for the rest of your life, like my friendship with Helmut and Hella, or with Bully Buhlan – and with Jean "Toots" Thielemans.

I was sitting at the RIAS studio imagining I was once again in a Brazilian dance club when a gentleman, who I knew from his records and admired, walked in. The guitarist Toots Thielemans was called "Supertoots" in Rio de Janeiro and had been awarded "Musician of the Century" in his adopted country of America. This was justified, I thought. He was one of the most innovative guitar players ever and one of the greatest harmonica players to boot. Now he stood next to me, curious, and introduced himself in his distinguished, modest way. It was the beginning of a wonderful friendship. Toots often came to Berlin in those days, and I would always pick him up at the airport. I had him stay with us in our modest apartment. He showered, Gertraud fed him and he enjoyed being in a home instead of a hotel room. Sometimes he accompanied me to a gig and asked very carefully if he could join in. The impresarios and producers were always shocked by it; they were too intimidated to ask him. We played some songs for records and radio together. Among them were my compositions *Au revoir, mon amour* and Duke Ellington's *Caravan*. These two recordings later became hits of a special kind because a German company sold them worldwide as *Berieselungskassette* (background music). I would hear them years later at the

Jean "Toots" Thielemans with Adele Girard and Joe Marsala
Onyx Club, New York City, 1948
PHOTO BY WILLIAM P. GOTTLIEB, GOTTLIEB COLLECTION, LIBRARY OF CONGRESS

beach of a Holiday Inn in St. Lucia or in an elevator of the Waldorf Astoria in New York.

Curious, Toots once asked me if any money could be made writing songs. I told him about the combination of luck and feel for the times it requires. He became thoughtful. When I picked him up the next time at Tempelhof International Airport he pulled out the harmonica he always just happened to have with him and played a tune. He said: "That's my retirement!" He was right. *Bluesette* became an international hit. My friendship with Toots has lasted right up through today and has enriched my life.

Razzle Dazzle

I N THE SPRING of 1961, Gabbe's big band, together with the Roy Etzel band, were booked to play for the election campaign of Willy Brandt, who had been the mayor of Berlin since 1957. The Social Democratic Party had undertaken a major reorganization in an attempt to gain a broader base after Konrad Adenauer's party, the conservative Christian Democratic Union, had won an absolute majority two years earlier. They had decided to do their utmost to win acceptance for their program by making their campaigns more fun. They wanted to counter the conservative campaign of fear with a campaign that had more zing and one that instilled a more confident mood. I loved this assignment because Traute and I were anything but thrilled by the direction that politics had taken in our difficult native country. There were all sorts of protests against rearmament, against atom bombs and so on, but the nationalistic tendency was rearing its ugly head once more.

The Germans were outraged that Israeli agents had located and abducted Adolf Eichmann, one of the men responsible for the *Endlösung* (the Final Solution), in Buenos Aires in May of 1960. It was also appalling how small-time and even powerful former Nazis had gotten positions in government. Now they were deciding the fate of the people who had barely escaped the lethal atrocities committed during the Third Reich. No, despite the good mood we engendered from the stage every night I knew that what had happened twenty years before was not over and would never be over. I did not talk about it and did not show my feelings, but they were always present.

I still do not know how to handle it the right way: it cannot be forgotten, ignored or suppressed, but the remainder of your life should not be determined solely by the horrors that happened decades ago. I have played *La Paloma* countless times over the years, and sometimes I thought about the people who were being herded to their deaths. But there were times when I did not think of

Willy Brandt, mayor of Berlin, on the campaign trail for German chancellor. Coco Schumann partially hidden (right), 1960

them. I thought about the music. I had at least one good reason to never play *La Paloma* again, but I had a thousand reasons to play it: everyone in the audience of Willy Brandt's election campaign.

Brandt had a lot of charisma, understood how to stay in the news and was at the same time a "normal" human being and not just another politician like we have today. He believed in what he said and acted accordingly, and he knew how to convince others about it.

We had a lot of fun on that campaign tour with Roberto Blanco, Silvio Francesco and the shooting star of those days, Willy Hagara. We got along great, which meant we could not resist teasing each other – especially at performances. Roberto would sing a medley of his hits, and the audience went crazy when Silvio discovered a bicycle backstage and kept cycling back and forth while Roberto was in the middle of a medley of his hit songs. The place was cooking, and he was asking Roberto for directions! Roberto took his revenge the very next evening when Silvio started to warble his hit song *Mein Chapeau* (My Hat). Roberto found a handy stretcher, bandaged his head and had four workers carry him up on stage and put him down beside the microphone. Silvio was perturbed, meanwhile we were bending over laughing behind our instruments.

Things became serious only once. We were playing once again in one of the small towns, Roberto was singing his hit *Angel Negro* (Black Angel) and I was standing behind him playing my guitar. During the song, a man in the front row suffered an epileptic fit. I had never seen a black man turn white before, but Roberto did just that. He had to stop singing. He was so shocked that he could not sing anymore that evening. I was in a terrific mood the next evening because Willy Kettel had joined us, the old drummer from the *Rosita Bar*. I had been a fan of his when I was a boy and was still a fan even if he was now playing piano in some small hamlet. I guess the devil got into me that night because while Roberto was singing *Angel Negro* I tapped him on the shoulder, winked at him and acted like I was having an epileptic attack. He turned white again and had to stop singing! I think it would still work today, but I have been wise enough not to try it again.

The tour lasted for three months and was exhausting. We were rocking and rolling in a bus through the entire country. Sometimes performers would climb aboard and join us for just a few shows. The characters in the crew kept changing. One morning I got on the bus and discovered a new face I recognized right away. It took me a second to remember where I had seen it before. He had already recognized me, and we gave each other a hug. Boby John was a fairly well-known comedian whose most famous skit – *Herr Fröhlich und Herr Schön* (Mr. Happy and Mr. Nice)– had made me laugh even in Theresienstadt. He, on the other hand, had been touched by the performance of the young drummer who played with The Ghetto Swingers. We talked about the bad old days and the good times, too. We could not get over how lucky we had been to survive and to travel around in this country campaigning for the right man. We were in Bavaria one day, at the North Sea the next day and the day after that in the Allgäu. This is how I got to know Germany, even though not exactly to love it.

After a few weeks I had some problems with my health once again – the constant "memories" of my time in the concentration camps. Auschwitz-Birkenau and most of the winter nights spent on the cold clay ground at the Kaufering camp, combined with the typhoid fever I picked up as a result, had left its marks on me; I had to stop touring for a long time. The months I spent at the hospital were hell: rest, no smoking and spending the night in bed – altogether a catastrophe, not something you would wish for, not upon your worst enemy. At least I had time to do some thinking and used it to decide to become independent again, start my own combo and appear on radio and television. We began to rehearse shortly after Bubi Scholz, the Berlin knockdown/get-up guy from the *Sportpalast*, had lost his middleweight title after having made a hard-won comeback. We had our debut at the opening of the *New Eden Salon*, with its midnight shows, cabaret and dance numbers.

The combo was engaged at the *Palladium* for the winter season after the Gabbe Band had moved on. It was a huge venue that had the nickname "the house of a thousand club chairs" – but I think it was closer to five hundred. I was finally back in my old groove. Our contract obliged us to play until four thirty in the morning on Saturdays and until three o'clock in the morning on weeknights. The audience pulled out all the stops and went on a toot that is hard to imagine today. The joint was jumping.

Talent contests were all the rage. Some young people who came in every day had gotten it into their heads that they could become rich and famous without doing much. The result, despite a few contestants who had some talent, was horrifying. Sometimes though, somebody came along who had what it took. One evening a young girl named Manuela gave it a try. She was working in a factory and was encouraged by her boyfriend, who was called "Banana" because he was a fruit dealer. She was not half-bad, and the head of the Meisel-Musikverlag (Meisel Music Publishing House), the company I had done business with before, asked me to show her how to play guitar. It wasn't hard to teach her a few chords. Her first record *Schuld war nur der Bossa Nova* (Blame It on Bossa Nova) came out soon after that. At a similar singing contest at the *Neue Welt,* I had to follow the competition, this time from a seat on the jury. We awarded first prize to Drafi Deutscher, a really good singer. Somewhat later at the *Romanisches Café,* we accompanied a little girl who had shyly asked us earlier if we could play *Mamatschi, schenk mir ein Pferdchen* (Mamatschi, Give Me a Little Horse). We were only too happy to oblige, and of course Marianne Rosenberg won her first recording contract that night.

Berlin had long since become the capital of pop music in Germany again. Every evening brought new attractions. The supposedly best show band in Europe played the *Palladium,* and some of the hype turned out to be true. In the ballroom of the Hilton Hotel we danced the twist like we were being paid for it, with the Rebel Guys and the Team Beats, while the TNT combo from the Netherlands presented the top attraction, the *Linda Lu Bademodenschau* (Linda Lu Swimsuit Fashion Show). Those were the days – marvelous times of economic miracles.

The new music "made in Germany" was becoming popular again. Everybody was talking about Helmut Zacharias, and Bert Kaempfert was considered a first-rate "hit maker" after releasing *Strangers in the Night* and *Moon over Naples.* About thirty-five hundred American disc jockeys voted his band to be the "Number One Orchestra of the Future".

In June 1963, John F. Kennedy assured us rather convincingly that he was actually one of us, a Berliner; and we, the Coco Schumann Combo, thanked him by signing a contract with the NCO club *Silverwings* as a "special service" for the Berlin brigade. Something was going on there every day: bingo parlors, dances, "Poor Boy's Nite" – happy hour for drinks that cost ten cents a shot. Unfortunately we could only play half of our program because melodies and numbers from the Soviet zone or communist countries were not permitted. "Speech or gestures derogatory against any member of NATO or the Federal Republic of Germany or the United States of America shall be considered grounds for termination of contract, in addition to insolence, drunkenness, smoking on stage as well as obscene, objectionable repertoire." That last bit was open to interpretation. As entertainment musicians, we were not in a good position; we were neither stars nor American.

At the beginning of 1964, I dissolved my combo and founded my new Radio and Record Quartet with Wolfgang Kuntze on bass, Günter Mozer on drums, and Rolf Sztuka on piano and one of the first Hammond organs in Berlin. Our debut took place at the *Drugstore* on Kurfürstendamm. We quickly realized that we played well as a band, and we were offered a truly remarkable contract.

One Friday evening in spring of 1964, I stepped into the *Kasino am Zoo*, a large, modern club on Budapester Strasse. I entered the room and was terrified – nine customers sat here enjoying the view of the Memorial Cathedral. Any club could be on the outs at any time – even overnight. But knowing that did not help us much. We needed work, so I signed for the weekends for a period of two months, not without hearing as I left: "Good luck Mr. Schumann, but don't have any false hopes. You aren't going to have a crowd on Fridays."

Eight weeks later I stood in the office to see about a renewal of our contract. "What's wrong with you today? It's Friday and there's only a hundred and fifty people there!" We played and kept the place filled with customers and stayed, with only a few interruptions, for a total of three years.

So we learned how hard it can be when you have to be the life of the party. We played everything that was suitable to keep the place hopping – from rare old swing titles to the newest Arab earworm, from Hungarian ballads to Rhineland carnival hits. I have to confess that I had a ball. I never had a problem with the supposedly low level of musicianship of certain kinds of music. There was only one thing that mattered to me: the quality of the song and its effect on the audience. Most of the time they were thrilled, whether we sang Russian, Turkish, American, Brazilian or Norwegian songs – which we did only phonetically – an

Coco Schumann and his new Radio and Record Quartet with Wolfgang Kuntze on bass, Günter Mozer on drums and Rolf Sztuka on one of the first Berliner Hammond organs *Drugstore* on Kurfürstendamm, Berlin, 1964

exercise that, once mastered, can win you a lot of admiration. The best one in this regard was our bass player, Wolfgang Kuntze.

The days we spent at the *Kasino am Zoo* were happy days, and the booze was flowing. You might say those days went to our head. I have already mentioned that we did not play in alcohol-free clubs. In other words, sometimes we drank like fishes, an integral part of our business. After our gig was over, we would leave the club in a state of spectacular inebriation and frequent a bunch of other clubs. From time to time, we created havoc in the early morning rush hour traffic and left sensible people scratching their tired heads after watching our antics.

As enjoyable as these final notes were, over time they created a certain amount of dissonance. Drinking became a problem for some of us, and as much as alcohol initially enlivened some careers, it took its toll on many musicians as time went by. I do not know many musicians who realized what was happening to them and who, as a result of this insight, stopped drinking.

Drinking was at times a specific problem for me, but it was never a threat to my career. No two people are alike. I rarely came home after work without having drunk at least a bottle of schnapps. I could do without it anytime I wanted to, however. I stopped having fun drinking and would have water for the rest of the evening. I have not been able to drink for a long time now, but that has not bothered me one bit. Countless tempting glasses have passed me by.

When I listen to the recordings from the *Kasino am Zoo* today I am surprised at the range of styles we offered. The idea was to bring together the various interests of the colorful audiences. As is well known, hits come and go in a hurry. We would hear a new hit on the radio sometimes and were playing it the very next day, which left our customers astounded and bewildered at times.

You need to have a lot of feeling for the way an evening unfolds, too. Playing a wonderful hot jazz number to the right crowd at the wrong moment you will crash and burn. If you wait for the right moment, maybe just half an hour later, everybody will cheer. You have to watch your audience like a hawk in order to know them – and to like them. When you are a live performer you have a duty to your audience. They work all day long to earn a little fun at a club. You cannot keep them at arm's length; you have to sense what they need from you. If you can do that you can allow yourself to be surprised and to be able to develop your own style from the various types of music you need to play. I believe our quartet was able to do that back then.

All the different trends in music were still moving alongside each other, with each other, something I personally enjoyed. Except for country music and German folk music, I liked everything that was good, as long as I understood it. I did have some problems with the new directions jazz was taking. At the *Jazzgalerie*, a club on Bundesallee, I was stopped in my tracks when I heard free jazz. I just could not get into it. They asked me to join in, and I climbed up half-heartedly on stage in my white suit and played something I was not entirely convinced of. The audience applauded and seemed to like it, but this kind of music left me cold even though excellent musicians were playing it. My kind of improvisation stemmed from a very different strain that ran back to a different world. It had almost nothing to do with the kind of self-expression that was required here. A lot of my friends, even those who were not musicians, felt the way I did. The jazz scene began to disappear and reappear at the same time. I had a special fondness for the cool style of Dave Brubeck, Paul Desmond, Gerry Mulligan and Astrud Gilberto, whose music I loved, whose way of feeling melodies was close to my own. The same was true about Jimi Hendrix; I had a certain admiration for his skills, but I didn't try to emulate him because I didn't want to bite into my expensive guitar.

I had modified my Hoyer guitar by adding special pickups and a circuit for special effects I needed for the *Kasino*, for sirtaki and other exotic stuff. I appeared with this modified monster guitar at a concert of the Swedish group the Spotniks, whose signature sound was a spacey guitar with lots of reverb, a sound similar to the Shadows. One of the promoters recognized me and asked me onstage. We improvised my song *Rockin' Guitar.* All hell broke loose in the club, and I stayed with them for the rest of the evening. The Spotniks played lots of cover versions of chestnuts from every provenance, something that suited me perfectly. So we played a smoking rock version of *In the Mood* and an astronaut version of *Habanera* from Bizet's *Carmen.* After the Spotniks played their interpretation of *Ku'damm Promenade,* we played a contemporary electric version of *Hava Nagila,* something I particularly enjoyed. There are at least as many outstanding versions of this beautiful song as there are of *La Paloma.*

In the spring of 1965 – a week before Cassius Clay would win the world heavyweight title for the first time against Sonny Liston – we went back on tour for Willy Brandt, with a coterie of stars. He had just been elected as party leader of the Social Democrats. We started off our show with *Skinny Minnie, Stupid Cupid* and *Razzle Dazzle,* then changed tempo with *Berliner Luft* (Berlin Air), leaving the crowd hanging by the ropes before Willy finally stepped onto the stage. When all was said and done, we were not able to prevent Ludwig Erhard from becoming the next chancellor of Germany.

Then I met Bubi Scholz, the retired boxer who had bought for his wife Helga a chain of cosmetic shops that sold beauty products and had opened a PR agency for himself to market his popularity as an actor and singer. He was looking for a good band for his nightclub called *Red Rose* at the Europa Center. He made us an offer we could not refuse, so we spent an exciting fall and winter playing a truly fascinating show that had stars from the *Casino de Monte Carlo* and the *Paris Lido,* with the Hovens, comedians from Las Vegas; Jackie France, the "Mannequin de la nuit"; Kiki Omnibus from the *Crazy Horse* and Nadja Nadlova from Brussels who were quite convincing taking it all off in their final number "Intimate Finale". One of the ladies called herself Natascha. When she undressed, her legs just wouldn't end, but when she opened her mouth her Saxon accent would stop you in your tracks. A good striptease isn't easy, and it is not indecent. It's an art form, or, in other words, it was – because this business has undergone its own dramatic change. Anyway, whenever I think about playing the *Red Rose,* I remember a first rate gig.

We played during 1970 in more or less the same way. A world-class program was announced in the *Daily Girl Club* – along with the so-called "Krabben-Service" (crab service) with a dozen "topless girls", featuring artists and illusionists from old-school variety shows.

In the meantime, our quartet was cruising all around West Berlin.

Coco Schumann and his quartet at the *Red Rose*
Rolf Sztuka, Günter Mozer, Coco Schumann and Wolfgang Kuntze, 1965

We played the *Töff-Töff*, the *Club 50* and *Bal Paré*, the club that replaced the legendary *Casaleon* on the Hasenheide where I had played when I was just a kid. There is a pizza place there today called *Casaleon,* so the old days have not been completely forgotten. We would return to the *Kasino am Zoo* every once in a while to stabilize the numbers of customers on Friday evenings.

Since we had never made it "bigtime", I enjoyed being a craftsman. I could feed my little family. On the other hand, I had a burr under my saddle that caused me to wonder if there was a life after Berlin, with all the comforts it offered. I had not made much effort to stay in touch with musician friends who lived in other parts of the world. The two occasions when I tried to organize a gig at the officers' club in Tripoli and a top hotel in Tunisia did not work out financially. Traute and I were not able to realize our secret dream of moving to America, perhaps because we were not courageous enough and certainly because we did not have the financial requirements.

So the only thing for us to do was to be happy about an engagement my quartet got in the summer of 1968, a featured gig at the *Romanisches Café* that lasted for several months. It was one of the Blatzheim Group's outlets, which meant the gig was solid and secure – as long as we followed their strict rules and did not cause any trouble. We were well-behaved, hardworking, obedient and avoided anything that might cause us to miss a performance. We kept our wild side on a leash until we were off work. We were relocated the following spring, something a company like Blatzheim had in their contract and made use of with us. I had not read the small print when I signed the contract. The famous *Park Café* in Munich had lost a lot of its audience and caused the management a lot of worry. They thought we were just what the doctor ordered. Soon after our arrival however, we had to follow tough rules. A stiff wind was blowing. We had our pride and played up and down the top forty hit list the way we always did for the afternoon tea dance and evenings. Kuntze's father owned a bed and breakfast in a small town called Reit im Winkl, so Wolfgang had a terrible Bavarian accent that highly amused the customers.

We played our best, and we were exemplary otherwise as well. After repeated requests to be on time we had ourselves a little fun. We put Rolf Sztuka's watch onto the Hammond organ and agreed on a couple of secret signs. We began at four in the afternoon sharp and stopped at six, regardless of where we were in a given song. Every time, the waiters' jaws dropped to the floor, and we were amused. After a week, the headwaiter whispered to us that management had told them, "Please set your clocks when Mr. Schumann starts his shift!" After another week the headwaiter stammered, "Gentlemen, this has never happened before. Herr Direktor wants to know what you would like to drink."

Finally I asked the regional manager for a pay raise, something that was regarded as a very bold thing to do at Blatzheim. In our case, my request was immediately granted. However, the new contract stipulated, "You do not have any right to make any further requests, and you will not do so." Jawoll! I was never as happy as I was when this gig finally came to an end.

The times had become darker. People were not as carefree as they had been before. A lot of old clubs had closed their doors for good, others could not afford to hire a band, even radio appearances dwindled away. I was torn between the reliable and still successful performances of my quartet and toying with the idea that the future might offer a completely different set of challenges.

The mood in the nation was not the best. West Germany began to flirt with extremism again; the *Nationaldemokratische Partei Deutschlands*, the NPD (German Nationalist Party), had become a factor in the political spectrum. I was not too happy with what the extreme left wing was coming up with, either. I sometimes thought I could recognize the "game" from my youth. I was depressed. To make things worse, Rocky Marciano, the former heavyweight champion of the world, was killed in a plane crash. The Social Democrats

"To be able to live in peace tomorrow. SPD" – a campaign poster for Willy Brandt's successful bid for German chancellor, 1969. Brandt was awarded the Nobel Peace Prize in 1971.
COURTESY: BUNDESARCHIV

informed me that they had decided they were going with a more "factual" style – which was too bad for us but proved to be successful in the end. Willy Brandt was finally elected chancellor in October of 1969.

Despite the election results, Traute and I thought more seriously about leaving Germany again. Of course we included in our plans my favorite old uncle Arthur, with whom we had kept in touch over all these decades. He and his first wife Edith had been clever enough to leave Germany – unlike the rest of my family – as a reaction to the events of November 9, 1938, Kristallnacht. At the time I could not understand why they left and was disappointed, because I loved both of them. His decision, however, had contributed to my becoming a jazz musician because he left me his drum set. He never found his way back to music – there was too much going on.

After his arrival in La Paz he had handed brilliant-cut diamonds to a friend who worked at the Bolivian delegation in Berlin because he could transport them in his diplomatic pouch. He did, but then the friend took off with them.

This was Uncle Arthur's first bitter disappointment. My uncle and aunt had to start over with what they had left: a trunk full of evening wear, including that white tuxedo.

As a true man of the world, Arthur did not have any problems figuring out how to get out of a situation. He opened a small barbershop in Cochabamba with an adjoining bar that quickly became the hangout for a lot of emigrant ex-Berliners who in turn became regular clients at the shop. They had changed continents but not their hair stylist.

He started a sideline as a smuggler – of shoes. They were extremely expensive in Bolivia, but not in neighboring Peru. He used his exotic Mediterranean skin tone, made himself up like a Latin American guy, put on some old clothes, worn-out shoes, crossed the border and headed for Lake Titicaca. When he returned at night, he was searched top to bottom by the Bolivian custom officials. Although they suspected he was smuggling something they could never figure out what it was. Arthur traveled home across the Bolivian highlands with his new shoes and had made a nice cut once again.

Soon Edith and he had earned enough to move to North America to start a chicken farm near New York. That did not work out as hoped because some disease wiped out the dear feathered friends. By the time the war was over, they had wound up in midtown New York. My uncle bet the farm and opened yet another barber and beauty salon on Fifth Avenue that boasted five lovely display windows and a real novelty à la Arthur: an adjoining dry cleaner. His illustrious customers – Perry Como, a crooner, was a regular – wore bathrobes while getting their haircut. As soon as the haircut was finished, so was their dry cleaning.

The shop was a hit, and both of them became wealthy. Arthur changed over to real estate and did well investing in skyscrapers. After the death of his wife, he became restless once again. He wanted to know what life was like in the "new" Europe. He settled in Switzerland and then in Israel, but neither place suited him. He moved to Miami with his second wife Rita.

Once a year, he visited his former native land and us. He has done it ever since. He turns ninety-four this September and is looking forward to each new day just as he has always done.

We thought about his life and his destiny while we were mulling over whether to stay in Berlin or leave. We could not make up our minds and lacked the safety net. I did not and still do not have my uncle's spirit of adventure.

Dosvedanje

I MET MY OLD FRIEND Bully Buhlan again in the spring of 1970. I was going about my business, playing for the Jewish community, bar mitzvahs, tea dances and similar gigs, and, somewhat halfheartedly, at the *Romana* restaurant on Kurfürstendamm.

However, Bully told me something that would lead to a change of scenery over the coming years. Even he had to struggle for the past couple of years, so he had "gone to sea" to play on cruise ships. At first I was horrified because my seafaring experience was limited to stuffy sea trips to Denmark and back to buy duty-free goods. These cruises, Bully immediately explained, were not like that at all. They had high standards, even if the large German travel company Neckermann had tried to get "normal" tourists on board. It didn't appear this venue was the worst place to play. I sent some selections from our recordings to an agency he recommended.

They called me the next day and said if we wanted to come it would be really sensational. They did not have to ask twice. Another attraction of this line of work was the fact that I could feel the wind in my face again and take a little "holiday away from home".

On March 26, 1970, our quartet boarded the *Taras Shevchenko* in Genoa, as part of a crew of three hundred and seventy men. It was one of the most modern ocean liners in the world at that time, built in Odessa under the flag of a Black Sea shipbuilding company and now chartered by Neckermann for German tourists who wanted to make a round trip through the Mediterranean and the Orient. Neckermann had made a lucky draw. The ship made a powerful impression on its seven hundred and fifty passengers with its length of one hundred and eighty meters and diesel engines that generated twenty-eight horsepower for each of its seven hundred and fifty passengers. It was outfitted with opulent interiors, and on top of that, it was an altogether elegant vessel. Nine decks held comfortable cabins

Artist postcard for the Coco Schumann Quartet
Rolf Sztuka, Coco Schumann, Günter Moser and Wolfgang Kuntze, no date

and various social rooms, dining halls, swimming pools with glass ceilings, cinemas, music salons, smoking rooms and – most importantly for us – five bars.

When the steward showed us around the ship and explained our place in the scheme of things on board – we enjoyed the status of "special" employees and hence the same service offered to passengers – we felt right at home. We carefully reassembled the Hammond organ again, which we had elaborately taken apart for its transportation, and did not mind being part of this large dream machine. The ship was named for the revolutionary Ukranian poet Taras Grigorovich Shevchenko, who had been in trouble with the Czar all of his life and died in 1861 at the age of only forty-seven. Our ship nicely combined Russian style and a sharply curtailed socialist ideology with the needs of several hundred capitalist tourists and their desire for entertainment and relaxation. After an initial slight anxiety upon first contact with the "red menace", they had no problem enjoying the charm and luxury. They could not have known that the captain of the *Taras* had commanded a Russian warship at the Bay of Pigs not too long ago. A number of the crew had probably been on that warship the day the "free western world" had been humiliated – who knows? On cruise ships, it is customary for the crew to have as little contact with the passengers as possible. The Soviets did not like to see their comrades fraternize with the class enemy.

Coco Schumann Quartet at a costume party on the *Taras*
Coco Schumann, Rolf Sztuka, Günter Mozer and Wolfgang Kuntze, 1970

I did not have to go far to get from my four-bed first class cabin that was assigned to me and other band members to our workplace, the *Ukraine Bar*, which was located high above the bridge deck, the nicest place on the ship. The interior decoration consisted of Ukrainian folk art, and the bar offered a selection of the finest vodkas and Armenian, Ukrainian and Moldavian cognacs. The tailor shop on the second deck below added the final touches to our outfits, and we were good to go. This was more than a little absurd; after the care we had to take when playing music from the east at the *Silverwings Club*, we were now able to drink from a full cup and stir the emotions and passions of the passengers and, most especially, the officers. When we left the Spanish harbor of La Coruña, we were asked to play on deck with the ship's Russian band. I suggested playing the Russian evergreen *Dosvedanje*. We were astonished to discover our colleagues did not know how to play it. After a few minutes we handed them copies of our arrangement and proceeded to undertake a curious "meeting of cultures" . . .

Two days later, the first officer interrupted us just before the evening was over, at four thirty in the morning, and said: "Coco, wrap it up – the captain wants to talk to you. Tonight, you'll have to drink." Fortunately, I had been getting along okay with Mascha, the Russian stewardess at the bar. She pulled me into the kitchen and stuffed me full of all sorts of fatty things – sardines and so on. On my way to see the captain! He had heard that while my fellow countrymen had besieged Stalingrad, I had been in a concentration camp. He wanted to show his respect, a respect that became high esteem during the course of the morning when I was able to stay on my feet downing sixty-proof "Starka Vodka" and drank the entire staff of command under the table. Our relationship became very close over the remainder of the cruise – and very exhausting.

I got to know the political officer the next evening and told him: "You know, capitalism is bad – very, very bad!" He looked up from his glass, scooted over to my side and said: "You're right, Coco. Bravo!" He looked over to the bar: "Hey, another schnapps for Coco!" We clinked our glasses together, and I continued my diatribe: "But a million in your pocket is *ochen korosho* (very nice), right?" He sized me up and grinned: "A million in your pocket is *ochen korosho!* Hey, another schnapps for Coco!" And so on.

A shot of schnapps cost about thirty cents and a cocktail that had the charming name *tschernomorotschka* cost about one mark eighty. A lot of the passengers were not used to these conditions and could be found lying in the hallways while the evening was still young; others staggered out of the bar early in the morning and fell asleep in the museums or ruins that were on the program for that day. We usually left the bar at around eight in the morning. If we did not head straight for the sun deck, forcing the sailors to sweep the decks around our chairs, we stuck our heads out into the warm Mediterranean breeze with a thick La Corona cigar in our mouths. We thought life was good.

I got along particularly well with one of the officers, Wassilij. We were both responsible for introducing new passengers to the ship's protocols. The fresh passengers were sitting in one of the bars, getting to know things after they had been assigned their cabins, still somewhat shy. The Russian uniforms were foreign to them and caused them to feel somewhat uncomfortable. Wassilij and I were sitting at the bar, waiting until the ship set sail. We began to chat in a loud voice:

"Mr. Schumann, have you heard the news today?"

"No, why?"

"It just came in over the radio. Strauss is a Russian spy!" (Strauss, an archconservative CSU party leader.)

"Oh my God!" The tourists were shocked.

"And he's probably a Jew!"

While all hell broke loose inside, we waited outside on the deck, leaning against a lifeboat, bent over with laughter. It worked every time!

Our daily routine at sea was pretty habitual, but a spirited and freewheeling program added diversion and meaning. Programs put on by the Russian administration alternated with its "ideological" counterpart, the shows and the fun courtesy of the Neckermann company. After breakfast, you could take a Russian language course followed by a presentation at the cinema hall: "Financial instruments – an interesting way to invest!" This in turn was followed by a morning drink and accompanied by the Russian orchestra, a slide show about Morocco and a chess game at the library. You could play bingo during tea, and advanced students could dance rumba on the upper deck. The cinema filled in the intervals until dinner and the gala evening at the great salon with a Russian orchestra, a comedy trio and us. For the finale, we went back to the *Ukraine Bar* and played the hits on the Neckermann hit list until night turned to day.

We were able to master every situation with our music. The Egyptian secret police boarded our ship in Malta to keep an eye on the passengers as we were heading for Alexandria. Battles were being fought in the Suez, and there were terrible battles between Israel and the United Arab Republic. I was worried because my second Christian name Jakob was included in my passport. I got the boys ready to play that evening.

Wolfgang Kuntze had a previously mentioned gift – he could sing songs in other languages without understanding them. It was a purely phonetical aptitude that required a good ear and some imagination. He had become a member of the Islamic faith, had studied the Koran and could pray for hours and hours – he sometimes sang at the mosque on Hohenzollerndamm – so he was in his element. When some mysterious gentlemen entered the bar, we played an Arab top hit of those days, *Ayasin*. They were so thrilled, their ears fell off. They had not expected something like this.

When we sailed into the heavily defended harbor of Alexandria, I was immediately summoned to the immigration department. I did not feel very well until the police officers greeted me, laughing. I was introduced as the leader of a German-Arab band. "Jakob" did not matter to anyone. From then on I was greeted by my new friends as soon as the *Taras* docked at the pier.

I had no understanding of the three wars and the ongoing confrontations between Israel and its neighbors: Lebanon, Syria, Jordan and the United Arab Republic. That was probably because I did not have any understanding of war, and I did not want to understand it. I felt an inner bond with Israel and had toyed with the idea of moving there. The radicalism I saw there stopped me. Orthodox Judaism would not have been my cup of tea because I do not like others telling me what to do.

The way Israelis and Palestinians treat each other to this very day is atrocious. Perhaps I am being politically naive, but I have lost relatives to "terrorists" myself. The wars in the Near East were not and are not my wars. No war is my war. I have lots of friends among the Arabs and the Jews, and I love to play both Jewish and Arab music – that's the only thing that counts for me.

So, we were on deck in a great mood. We were young, boisterous, and that is how we felt. There was not a moment we didn't have for a more or less decent joke. There was not a day we weren't ready for some silliness. We spent the port calls wearing a full-length kaftan or burnus that we had picked up at a bazaar. The hours we spent on the sun deck had caused us to look somewhat more oriental – something that at times resulted in curious events.

One of my days off I spent on deck. We had dropped anchor in Istanbul. Some passengers who had returned from their outing told me that my three kids Günter Mozer, Kuntze and Rolf Sztuka were standing in the middle of a bazaar totally covered up in Arab garb playing flutes and tambourine on the street – Turkish music, of course, with the locals showering them with coins.

While the ship was making ready to sail the next afternoon, already running late, we noticed that Kuntze was missing. We begged the first officer to wait for him. The loss of our bass player and vocalist would have been a disater for us. We waited nervously at the railing. Nobody in sight. Suddenly a motorcycle came racing down the pier, the passenger in a swaying kaftan and bouncing fez hurried up the gangway. They did not want to let him on board, which set off a ferocious quarrel during which we recognized Kuntze's voice – though even we had not recognized him by sight. He had been in a mosque praying and had gotten lost on the way back until the motorcycle guy took pity on him.

Just before our arrival in Beirut, they warned the passengers and us not to buy any hashish on our outing because if we were caught the punishment would be draconian. Nobody would be able to help us if we landed in prison. We put in at the harbor with the most fragrant spices of the Near East, and I strolled down the gangplank. I saw a few policemen standing down there and felt the devil in me. I walked straight up to the gentleman with the most stars on his shoulders and asked "Excuse me, Sir, can you tell me where I can buy some hashish?"

He looked at me as though I was from another planet and was about to reach for his holster. Apparently I was grinning so stupidly that he started to laugh uncontrollably. He called his colleagues over. I had to repeat my question until they were all bending over laughing hard. We became best friends, and he taught me a lot of terrible Arab curses that I was able to put to good use to shock the Arab traders if they started dickering with some fantasy prices at the bazaar.

The boys and I had made a name for ourselves at the harbor district in record time, and they were waiting for us every time the *Taras* docked in Beirut. I even knew a taxi driver, Paul, who was there only for us as long as we were at the harbor. He introduced me to his entire family the second or third time we anchored there. In the living room of his second wife, he fished out a package and handed it to me as a gift. I unpacked it on board later on – it was red Lebanese! I had tried a lot of different kinds of drugs in my time, with varying degrees of pleasure, but this hashish soon proved to be the best ever. The passengers on the *Taras* were having fun their first evening in Beirut at the *Casino de Liban*, then one of the best variety shows in the world, much better than the *Moulin Rouge*. We had the night off and decided to try out the stuff.

The *Casino* closed a little earlier than usual. Suddenly the passengers streamed back on board. We were called to play the packed *Ukraine Bar* on short notice and crawled up onto the bandstand. When I tried to set the tempo, I saw the insanely grinning faces of my colleagues and could not stop laughing. The music we played was ethereally slow, impossible to dance to and, only for us, a tremendous expansion of consciousness. The performance was the worst catastrophe of my career.

Even though Gertraud could come along with us on two of the cruises, and though we had the best cabin on the ship – above, on the boat deck up front – the permanent separations over the years had placed a strain on our marriage. As adventurous and entertaining as the cruises were for me, I missed Traute – and she was missing me even more, sitting alone at home. In spring of 1972, I decided it was best to let my contract with Neckermann run out.

I had gotten out of touch with Berlin during my adventures in the Orient. Fewer and fewer clubs could afford a live band. Most of them were converted to discos, and what few good jobs there were were taken. I was not even sure if people wanted to listen to my combo. What opportunities were out there? I did not even want to think about resuming my career as a plumber, but the only thing I had learned besides playing some guitar was drinking.

That was it! If all else fails, go into politics or open a bar. I decided to open up a club of my own; it would be a leg to stand on and money for my retirement. I got in touch with some old friends who were at home in this business. The owner of the *Bal Paré*, an architect, had interesting leasing projects available that he built with plywood. He helped me find a cozy little shop on Giesebrechtstrasse that needed some fixing. It had previously been a Persian restaurant, a wild place where machine guns could be bought in the kitchen. A hand grenade must have fallen into the french fries because the ceiling was covered with an inch of grease.

We scrubbed the place for a few days and tossed some plaster onto the walls to make it look more Spanish. After a lot of mulling things over and innumerable suggestions we decided on the only name possible: the *Coco Bar!* I jumped right into the life of being a club owner. We put up a large photograph of me carrying beer mugs on the front door. If that did not attract customers, nothing would. I wanted all of my old acquaintances from the scene to come hang out at my place, so we opened the first evening at ten. All the other places had closed by then. They all came to check us out: waiters and disc jockeys, musicians, boxers and even a few characters from the demimonde – it was exactly the way I had imagined it.

I could finally satisfy another one of my passions. Together with my Lebanese cook, I would prepare simple dishes that had a special kick – "old Swedish recipes" laced with some Arab touches. The waiters from the steak houses curbed their appetite so they could come over and eat my top-secret steak recipe, the musicians got their stews and soups, the owners and their waiter staff had their drinks and the prostitutes stopped by, entirely welcome, to warm themselves on cold winter nights. I knew the ladies from my inquisitive walks through the Barnyard Quarter, from the time I spent in jazz cellars and bars, and I always liked them. Their profession is not worse than any other. Their pimps knocked politely at the door and asked if it would be okay for them to come in. None of them ever behaved badly at my place. If somebody was looking for a fight, the others would grab him by the collar and take him out into the street. They would make it clear to him that starting a fight was okay anywhere else, but not at Coco's!

Everything ran smoothly for a while. We were busy. Often the phone would ring at four in the morning. It was the *Café Keese*: "Don't close just yet, all of us are coming over with the johns." Those were big spenders, guys who were hungry and who liked to hang out with waiters so they could have some fun. They were customers who could be taken to the cleaners. Well, that is how the business works. The club did so well that instead of the orderly life we had planned, we got just the opposite. Some days I closed at high noon and had to start cooking goulash and sauerkraut again while Gertraud cleaned up the joint and polished the glasses.

After a few months, we were exhausted. Just as I was pounding spices into steaks, the telephone rang and Fräulein Fischer from Neckermann's chirped into my ear: "Coco, I have the list for next year ready for you. You can choose which boat you want to sail on. We do need you for the *Taras* for sure, this Christmas in the Caribbean. Buhlan will be on board, you're the only one who can accompany him."

I smiled and said: "How am I supposed to do that? Those days are over. I have a pub now, and I can't leave." She waited for me to finish: "Oh Coco, just look out the window. What's the weather like there?" It was a gloomy, cold November day, and rain was coming down in buckets. "Okay, send me the paperwork. I'll do it."

That's how Gertraud and I wound up a short time later in Genoa. Once again we got the best cabin on the ship and celebrated the best Christmas and New Year's Eve ever since the night we were at the American hotel. We sailed around close to the small but beautiful Isla del Coco – traversing the Panama Canal and bearing a thousand kilometers to the right – while back at the small but beautiful *Coco Bar* on a side street off Kurfürstendamm, with snow and sleet and the smell of salt-covered ice, things were going straight downhill. We had found someone to take care of the bar, and they ran it right into the ground. It was probably for the best.

While the *Taras* was anchored in Trinidad, Bully joined me at the swimming pool and said there was an organist sitting at the *Black Sea Bar* who wanted to talk to me. Even though an all too typical American was waiting for me there I recognized him immediately: John Hansen. We had played a jam session together right after the war was over, at the *Faun* at the Dammtor railway station. We gave each other a big hug. He had made career in America but sometimes also played on cruise ships.

Just before the cruise was over, we met again in Casablanca. John was playing the *Hamburg*, a ship that was owned by the Atlantic Line, and since this company knew about my combo from hearsay and by word of mouth via the enthusiastic passengers who had sailed the *Taras*, they seized the opportunity and told John to nab me for the next cruise. He asked me if I would like to play the *Hanseatic,* a real luxury liner built by a company in Hamburg. It carried American tourists from Fort Lauderdale through the Caribbean. After my hopes of earning some serious money with my guitar had been awakened, and with visions of a Caribbean dream vacation in the back of my head, I signed a nine-month contract on the *Hanseatic* in the autumn of 1973. We went on board in Cuxhaven shortly thereafter. When we slipped into Fort Lauderdale at the Everglades we were playing on the top deck for the occasion. I caught a glimpse of Uncle Arthur waiting on the pier. He had come over from Miami, over twenty-five miles away, just to see me. We embraced each other and were both happy about the reunion.

The *Hanseatic* was a little older than the *Taras*, but with its twelve decks it was bigger and more comfortable. The *Hamburg Salon* on the salon deck where we were going to play held two hundred and seventy passengers, and the rest were scattered around in the other establishments where Mia and the Sunny Boys, John Hansen and Bud Kurz provided entertainment.

The chefs in the kitchen were members of the *"Chaîne des Rôtisseurs"* (International Association of Gastronomy). The food was fabulous. Even breakfast offered fifty different selections. I believe the opulent midnight buffet was set up just for us musicians because the passengers were stuffed and the crew was not allowed to eat. I was simply unable to decide between smoked goose breasts or "wine grower style" young pheasant under glass, and I gained a substantial number of pounds. What did not concern me, but did impress me, was the availability of kosher meals and the "Sabbath service" early on Friday evenings. Well, my uncle lived in Miami, and so did a lot of other old Jewish immigrants.

We shuttled between Caracas, Grenada and Martinique, and every two weeks we returned to Port Everglade or Fort Lauderdale to pick up new passengers – otherwise life on board would have been boring. The daily grind was similar to the one on the *Taras*, only it was not as casual or boozed up. We played for international folklore evenings and "get-together-dances", harem parties, roaring twenties revues and all kinds of variety shows. I liked the diversity of people performing at these venues.

American entertainment is fundamentally different from German entertainment, not only because it's better, but also because nobody is too proud to make fun of themselves. The need for applause is different, too. Here in Germany, entertainers wait patiently and contentedly until the last round of applause has ended. They don't want to miss a single second of adulation, even if the show was a disaster. The American artists, however, start playing or singing in the middle of a burst of applause. They know they are good and do not need to wait for validation after every song.

Even the second and third string performers who had waited for years for Liza Minelli to break a leg were talented. They were often performing with no pay for their musical performances but instead got a free vacation out of it. What they did on that ship cannot be compared to the musicals we tried to put together. They just knew how to do it; they had the feeling. It was a great pleasure to play for them. I was finally able to experience my music the way I used to imagine it. Even the audience was better than on the *Taras*. Those were the VIP's and we were the VSOP's, the "very special operative people". Every cognac connoisseur will know what I am talking about, and the *Hanseatic* had a few damned good cognacs on board.

When we were back at our homeport in between voyages, John often played at the infamous Air Base No. One, an air force base and high security zone in Holmstead, where the most interesting nightclubs were located. The presidents of the United States came here to enjoy their privacy without any risk. John made sure that both of us, with Paul Pflanz on drums, could play there one evening.

It was fantastic to be successful with my own music after such a dry spell. The managers and officers of the club were beside themselves. When they learned that we were just passing through and normally played for tourists, and did not have the slightest chance to make a living from our music in Berlin, they urged us to apply for a green card on the spot so they could book us. But we hesitated – it was too sudden. We were back at the club the next time we were in our homeport. John introduced me to Al Telerico, the agent who ran the best hotels in Florida. According to rumor, he belonged to the mafia. There was something about the way he dressed and just stood there that made you believe it might be true. He parked his limo decorated with tiger skins in front of the door. It was so long that it wouldn't have even made it around a corner in Berlin.

I played a couple of Italian evergreens for him. He was beside himself with enthusiasm. Later he gestured for me to join him at the bar, and we talked for a little while until he finally asked: "Coco, you know who I am? I was your manager at the *Silverwings Club* in Berlin!" Our staff sergeant from Tempelhof – now I recognized him. He had not heard from me for a long time. My song *Exotique* had been a hit here in America in the sixties and was played by some big name musicians. Unfortunately, there was not much after that. He wanted to hire me on the spot and offered me a job at Marco Island, the finest hotel in Florida, located on a small island right across from Miami. This was a chance only the best of the best got in America, but I was not confident enough and turned him down.

As a consolation, something really nice landed in my lap. I was checking out the music shops of Fort Lauderdale with John and saw a Les Paul guitar, a fantastic instrument. I already had one, but the original Les Paul was so heavy that I was usually six inches shorter after a performance, which is why I did not use mine much anymore. John and I loved the sound, but I had a problem with the weight. The shop owner asked when I would be back. I told him I had to go to Jamaica and would return in two weeks.

When I got back I had a very special guitar waiting for me. It had a Japanese body but was much lighter than the American guitar. It also had a real Gibson neck and original pickups. Its sound was extremely nice and compared well with the original. Guitar buffs might complain that the neck was screwed on and not glued, but that did not matter to me. I was happy.

After two months in West Africa, the Mediterranean and the Black Sea, I stepped onto land in Cuxhaven and held Gertraud in my arms again. I had only seen her once in between cruises. She had been with me for a cruise of the Caribbean. Florida was like a dream for her, too. We were not certain whether we should move there for good. We finally decided to see about getting a winter domicile in Miami so we could have two summers, see Uncle Arthur more often and play some good music in the meantime.

In the following months, John and I wrote each other long letters and considered the situation. His wife Irene, who had worked on the *Hanseatic* as well, had landed a great job as the assistant to the general manager of the Ocean Reef Club, whose members had to have a net wealth of ten million dollars to join. The club offered us an engagement with top salaries, full service and an apartment on its grounds. John wrote: "*Also, Cocole, pack de Koffer und die Olle und komm geflogen, aber fix!*" (So, Coco, pack your bags and the old lady and catch the next plane, fast!)

This was something else. As much as we would have loved to leave Germany again the quickest way possible, it was not going to happen. Gertraud was not doing too well. She kept having problems that went back to the horror of the concentration camps, so we kept postponing the decision. By the time she had recovered from her latest bout, John's wife, Irene, had fallen ill, and John had accepted a cruise around the world.

Today, I think it would have been better if we had left immediately. It would have been better for the last years of our lives and better for my music.

We would not be sitting here in this country that is not my country anymore by now, a country to which I would not immigrate if I had the choice. Still, when I think about everything that has happened to me and everything I feel now, this is the place where I belong. I have made a lot of friends in this country and had some success. I have basked in the glow of human kindness here, too – enough to cause me considerable confusion. Sometimes I do not care about Germany. I just want to forget it. What counts are the people, the good and the bad. What counts is whether they pay attention to the way they treat each other and me. You just need to understand human failings.

I had to recall this when I met the famous composer Peter Kreuder on a cruise around the Mediterranean on the *Hanseatic*. He was playing the *Hansa Theater*, a cinema and theater auditorium at the bow of the ship. Kreuder's name was known all around the world. He had composed around a thousand songs and a hundred and fifty tunes for movies and had been the leader of a quintet in 1920 when he was a wunderkind of sixteen years. During the war, I did not know him yet and did not have a personal impression. Opinions about him were scattered all over the place. On the one hand, he was a first-rate jazz piano player – some even called him "the master of white jazz", a compliment he did not quite deserve. Among his fellow musicians, on the other hand, he was known for his vanity and for selling out.

His dealings with the National Socialists were ambiguous and dubious. He spread the rumor that he had been in South America during the war and had returned when it was over; however, he had joined the NSDAP (National Socialist) party in 1932. A large part of his popularity was due to the new mood that was sweeping the country at that time. He kept playing throughout the war, doing shows to entertain the soldiers and in motion pictures produced by the Nazi regime, including music used for their propaganda. His popular songs were highly regarded by Hitler and Goebbels. He briefly fell out of favor when he refused to perform in the heavily bombed Rhineland in 1943, but he was too valuable to be expelled from the Reichsmusikkammer. One might be permitted to observe that he was a master of naiveté.

So here we were, sitting at the bar talking about my unforgettable guitar teacher Hans Korseck, who was playing with Kreuder back then. We got sentimental about the old days, but every time it got a little "dicey", we changed the subject. There was not enough trust for questions about his thoughts during that period or about my experiences. I had an inner barrier to talking about those times. Everything else was okay; we talked like musicians do.

Sometimes I have to think about this conversation and about whether I had anything to reproach him for, and what I would have done if I had been in his situation. I do not know. If I wanted to play my music, perhaps as an Aryan I would have joined the party. After all, I had tried to become a member of the Reichsmusikkammer myself. The cross we had nailed in a classroom a long time ago to join the Hitler Youth was evidence of how quickly I could have gotten involved in the movement and then would have had a hard time getting out of it later on. I think we should not kid ourselves and think we are better than others. Most of us would have gone along back then, and most of us would go along with it today as well.

Autumn Leaves

B ACK IN GERMANY things were a lot quieter. I was at home more often than before. Of course, I took advantage of each opportunity to play in clubs, at the Jewish community centers, garden clubs or for company events, because I had to pay the bills. In 1975, I began to teach classical guitar at the Zehlendorf Conservatory.

The lessons and the attempt to share the secrets of the guitar with my students was, well, let's call it an "interesting" experience that gave me many happy moments. I had the feeling I was giving something back to their generation and doing something for music as well. There were many depressing moments, too, when a student could not realize his or her dreams – I mean the dream of becoming a "real" musician and not just playing the guitar. I did not learn to play the guitar at school, I learned how to play through life. I had the soul of jazz and swing in me when I sat at Uncle Arthur's drum set or when I tried to coax a few notes from the strings of my first guitar. Some of my students did not come to class with this sense of fun and excitement. They came with an instrument that could be exchanged with any other instrument. They came with the image of a life in music, or because their parents wanted them to. Some of them quickly learned what I showed them, sometimes overnight. But when they played it back to me I thought their ambition was to become a world champion typist! They had mastered three hundred error-free strokes per minute but did not know what it said in the letter they were typing. I could endure it when they played classical music, but with swing it was a no go: jazz does not allow for a dictatorship.

Notes are no more than black dots on paper. You can play them or you can bring them to life – then you do not need them anymore. Erroll Garner could not read music, but he was a marvelous musician all the same. He breathed life into music. When I listen to him, a chill runs down my spine. Django Reinhardt did not use sheet music, but nobody has even come close to playing like him. As much as I suffered sometimes during class, from time to time I was thrilled to discover a small, honest emotion, any swinging moment that a student would produce.

I had played with kindred spirits in all the bands and combos the previous decade, with friends for life who loved music. We kept track of each other, which means we spoke the same language and we could count on that. Helmut Zacharias told me early on: "Coco, you know what I'm going to play before I even play it." This is one of the secrets of swing. That's how it was with my bands. Even if we were playing elevator music or carnival standards, we had this in common, and it made up for the predictability of the music and made our performance something special for our audience. After a long time, actually from the very beginning, "normal" was something that was not normal at all, as I learned in Zehlendorf. Looking at it in this way, I went back to school again. It was an education that was sometimes sobering but was mostly refreshing and beautiful, and it let me see clearly what role music played and continues to play in my life.

In the late eighties, pop music began to change dramatically. The numbers I had spent my life with were not played nearly as often on the radio. The new way to appreciate music and to play it bothered me a lot. I did not keep my distance from the new music because of a fear of modernism but because it did not convey any emotion. There is nothing wrong in itself with being modern – after all, I was one of the first German electric guitar players and had even experimented with synthesizers. But the developing trend towards machine music was, with few exceptions, impossible for me to follow. For me, music is emotion, life, and machines do not offer either of the two. They are perfect and, above all, they never have what could be called mistakes. I make many mistakes when I play, and I make a lot of them because I like it – they prove that the music is alive.

Sometimes I listen to a new song on the radio while I'm shaving and think "Hey, not bad." After a few bars though, I start feeling uncomfortable. I do not know exactly why. But these electronic instruments give me a woozy feeling in my stomach. The monotonous drum machines hammer away, but they only make me feel like throwing up. Maybe I just don't get it; I'm too dumb to understand it? In the final analysis, it is an old game being played here. Our planet rotates around its axis, generally a good thing. Time takes no notice of the individual feelings of Coco Schumann or of the fact that I am getting older. I just come from another world; I have looked for and found a home in jazz. A home without nations, without inhuman value systems and without musical competition and short-lived attitudes. Today hardly anyone knows what a proper hully gully is, and in ten years something more modern will replace techno, but swing and the music of George Gershwin and Irving Berlin will still make its impact.

Many young musicians are on a sportive ego trip and play as though dynamic musical notation had never been invented. They play "faster, higher, louder" and what matters is who will be the first one to run through several thousand notes – as if music had nothing to do with feeling or eroticism. They start off loud, they don't get any quieter as the song progresses and come to an end with a loud bang without noticing what the other musicians in the band are playing. Everybody is playing a solo the whole time because everything can be fixed in the studio. In my opinion, good music lives because of its inner dynamic, the pauses, from playing quietly.

You only have to compare music with the other performing arts. What does some garden-variety Gretchen mean to me if she spits out her line "*Mein Ruh ist hin, mein Herz ist schwer*" (My repose is lost, my heart is heavy), or a Hamlet for whom "to scream or not to scream" is not even in question? This was actually the essence my only real teacher Hans Korseck gave me on my way: "Coco, it's important what you play, but what you don't play is even more important." Achieving a lot with a few notes. The less "performance" you deliver, the more room there is for feeling – and for the people you perform with. When we were jamming together at the *Badewanne*, Louis Armstrong sat next to me and listened to my improvisations. If it moved him, he laughed. If he had an idea, he took over. We simply played together, leaving each other space, composing for and accompanying each other. Accompaniment has become a lost art; for our music, it was the alpha and the omega.

One evening in 1985, we had again created a great vibe by playing everything the crowd wanted to hear. We had to perform the *Ententanz* (Dance of the Duck) four times in a row so the wife of the director, dressed in a little black nothing, could shake her behind. Around three or four o'clock, when the last customer slowly wobbled out of the establishment, we were hanging on by a thread at the bar and were obviously less than sober. All of a sudden I turned to my organist and said: "Lothar, I'm going to play only jazz again starting tomorrow!" Lothar gawked at me, laughed and ordered another schnapps. All of a sudden, I was sure in a way I had not been for years. This evening would be the last evening I was going to indulge other people's fancies, once and for all.

Things were not easy for the next couple of days. Out of the cabinet, I got my restored Gibson that I had found in a corner at Ace's in Miami covered with dirt and in bad shape, a Gibson 125. The first big band guitarists had played this instrument. I had scrubbed it clean, carefully and for several days. Finally I put on a coat of car polish to give it the wonderful finish it deserved. When I was done it looked as good as it sounded. I tried out some finger positions and rhythms that my fingers had almost forgotten. Sometimes I almost despaired when I tried to play some swing but couldn't get it into the strings.

But I had made up my mind. I was not the youngest kid on the block. In the time I had left, I was going to play what I enjoyed playing, period. I had tried to please others for as long as I could remember, friends and colleagues, for Helmut Zacharias, Wolfgang Gabbe and all the others, and had played *my* way what *they* wanted to convey to the audience. That was okay, I had fun doing it. But now I wanted to speak to them myself.

I have a lot to say. The direction was clear: back to the roots, back into the world where my soul was at home, swing. Into these mysterious, simple vibrations that musicians bring together and allow the spark to jump over to the audience; which, regardless of who they are or where they come from, makes everyone part of it. Anybody who has swing in his blood, whether in a dance hall or on stage, cannot march in lockstep any longer.

Back to the roots – that did not just concern the music. The more I got back my ability to get my fingering down and play the old frets and standards, the more I had the urge and the opportunity to improvise; the more I regained the ability to let my fingers, my head, my stomach and my soul play together, the more thoughts took hold that had not had a place in my everyday life for a long time. I had been playing for a good four and a half decades, and now music led me to reexamine my childhood and adolescence and to try to gain a few insights. I did not feel old with my barely sixty years, but I did feel somewhat more mature. I was confident about trying something I did not have the courage or the necessity to do during all those years: tell the story of my life.

The journalist Paul Karalus visited me in the summer of 1986. Together with Alfred Segeth, he planned to make a film about my life. I asked him which one he meant. He answered that he wanted both of them, that is, the one, the whole story. After all those years of keeping quiet, at first I was not ready to participate, but Karalus was able to convince me that it would not just be a new experience for me, it was my duty and obligation – to my own life, to music, to humanity. He made me think about why I had kept silent.

Those days would change my life. It had been forty-one years since I stumbled into the basement jazz club on Kurfürstendamm and startled my friends so much that their instruments fell out of their hands, as if my ghost had appeared in front of them. Perhaps it was at that moment that I asked myself what good it would do to explain more than saying the three words Theresienstadt, Auschwitz and Dachau; instead, I decided to grab my guitar and start playing whatever the new life offered. What good would it have done – I still do not know. I had found my old friends and my music, and I was afraid, I still was. Not of the Nazis, but afraid that I would not be a "German" anymore, not a musician, not a friend, just a victim, afraid I would hurt my friends and all those of whom I didn't know how they had conducted themselves, afraid to hurt or to bring shame. I was afraid that they would not want to have anything to do with me because they were embarrassed, and I was afraid that somebody would ask me how I could be in such a good mood after everything that had happened. Afraid of the anxiety, afraid of the loneliness that a fate like mine brings with it, and afraid of the images. Afraid of the nightmares about the camps and death, and afraid of the question why I had survived and so many others had not.

Over the course of time, something else came up: the realization that this country was not serious for one moment about whether justice was done, or about coming to terms with its own history; the impression that the guilty, the accomplices and the "innocent" criminals got off easily, were rehabilitated, placed in a good light, put into office and given honors and had the power to once again determine the lives of the "survivors". My friend, the writer Henryk M. Roder, made a penetrating remark a few years ago that I have not been able to forget: "Coco, they will never forgive us for what they did to us!"

I had kept quiet even with my close friends, Helmut, Hella, Bully and my musicians because I was living with them towards the future. The past had to remain the past; whoever knew about it, we understood each other without words. It took a few years for me to acknowledge the truth about my past and I felt I was ready now for the consequences: whoever had been in Auschwitz will never be able to leave, whether he wants to or not. It is impossible to forget; at some point you have to start to allow your memories to integrate into your life. While I do not believe in redemption, whatever may be its form, I do believe in the words of the writer Armin T. Wegner: "Wanting to forget prolongs the exile. The secret of redemption is memory." I had to find a way to talk about my life, just like I found a way to play La Paloma again.

A definitively true and authentic description of life and feelings at

Auschwitz is not possible, but each new attempt is an important part of the story that follows those times. A lot of survivors are still not able to come to terms with it or even to talk about it. Survivors still despair in retrospect. Whenever this happens to anyone, Hitler has won after all. The film by Paul Karalus was the beginning. I sat with Helmut and Hella at their home in front of a camera and began to speak to these two lovely people about what had happened in the death camps, these people I have trusted for years. I was not as afraid as I used to be because it was not about earning their sympathy but about finally telling my story. They were both shattered, but I knew they would understand what I was doing and agree with it.

To this day, I do not know how to convey to others in an appropriate way the things I saw and lived, but I do know I have to try. I do not want to upset people, I just want to tell it like it was. I do not believe in the collective guilt of Germans. I am a German myself, my parents were German and my grandparents were German – with their swords mounted on the wall, the grandfatherly huge Kaiser Wilhelm beard, always whistling a happy tune. How many of the estimated three million dead at Auschwitz-Birkenau and the countless other victims were – aside from everything else – German? Who cares about these distinctions, apart from the national socialist mass murderers and their successors? After all, many Germans helped me survive after my death sentence had already been pronounced; they gave me the chance to keep listening to my inner voice, a voice that has always been faithful and could tell me what to do.

After the first film *Coco, the Ghetto Swinger* was aired and after performances in jazz clubs and on the radio, people became interested in me again, at my old age, as a musician and as a witness of those times. The business about being a witness to history was not exactly easy. The more I talked, the more I recalled what I had deeply buried in my unconscious. Old dreams were haunting me. Remembering did not drive away the ghosts; it brought them on me like the hounds of hell. But by now I have learned to live with them without submitting to them or letting them distort my view of today and the future. My life, my joy in life – they did not get to it back then. I am not going to let them take it away from me now, even though the air has become thinner.

Traute and I kept thinking about whether to move to America or at least buy a winter home in Miami. We still had our suitcase packed and ready in the closet and enough money on hand to be able to drive to another country without having to go to the bank first. We never managed to jump over the pond, though. Gertraud got so sick that it was not realistic to think about moving. We stayed here and had to accept that we had reached a new stage in our lives: old age. Music became more important to me than ever before.

With my new quartet, we played the beautiful old standards: *Lester Leaps in, Let's Fall in Love* and *Girl from Ipanem*a. We found an audience that was willing to listen to the ballads I loved so much but had rarely played for a long time. This was jazz: on the one hand, life went on vigorously onstage, musicians laughing, telling jokes and teasing each other; on the other hand, there are these powerful, quiet moments when I want to embrace the whole world and get tears in my eyes. Take the song *Autumn Leaves* for example – *"The falling leaves drift by my window . . . And you can hear the old winter song . . ."*

Well, sure, the *Jefiehl* (feeling) was back again. A new scene began to take hold in Berlin for the kind of jazz we were playing. I talked about my music in all of the films and interviews that were suddenly being made about my life. From then on, I was the Ghetto-Swinger on stage. Both of my worlds had fused together and had become inseparable.

John Jeremy and Roy Ackermann made an English film called *Swing under the Swastika* in 1989. It contained interviews and documents about the history of jazz during the Third Reich. When Jeremy interviewed me he brought along a surprise: Martin Roman, the former leader of The Ghetto Swingers, came to Berlin and visited me at home. When we embraced each other I was overwhelmed. We spent several hours going through material that Jeremy laid out for me. We helped each other put it all together like pieces of a puzzle and found some of the pieces that we had forgotten over the years, or that I did not care to remember by myself.

The film was never shown here in Germany, but in America it has aired nationwide twice. That's how the veil was lifted for my American friends. One after the other, they called me up to talk about it. What I had not been able to speak about for decades became a moving experience – and provided incalculable publicity. Right after that I went into an old Schöneberg jazz club, the *Yorckschlösschen*, where one of Dizzy Gillespie's former drummers was playing. When he saw me he jumped up and called out "I know this guy from television in America! He's the man who played swing in a concentration camp . . ." and greeted me warmly. Well, this is something special, but it also goes to the heart of the matter: I am a musician, a musician who was imprisoned in a concentration camp, not a concentration camp inmate who also plays some music. The camps and the fear fundamentally changed my life, but it was shaped by music and music did its work well.

With Traute and Senator Volker Hassemer
at the award ceremony of the Order of Merit
of the Federal Republic of Germany
Europa-Center, Berlin, January 27, 1989

A letter from Senator Volker Hassemer arrived in January 1989, announcing it would be a great privilege and honor to award, in the name of the Federal President, the *Bundersverdienstkreuz* (Order of Merit of the Federal Republic of Germany) "in recognition of your outstanding achievements for the people and the state". At first I did not know what I should say except "wow" or something along those lines. Then I decided it would be a great honor and great fun to wear the medal – why not? The "special achievements for the people and the state" were subjective and formulated so vaguely that I could live with it. When I look at myself in the mirror, I do not see a man who has earned an order of merit. My songs, *Coco Nuts* or *Stripper Blues* were not special achievements of much import for German culture. I hoped, however, that the gentlemen had their reasons, so I accepted and got this thing hung around my neck for my decision to stay true to Berlin. I accepted it, thinking of the many people who did not receive this honor and could not receive it anymore. I accepted it in the name of music, with all the sense it made and all the nonsense, for all it restores day after day that has been destroyed by others.

Soon after I had resigned my teaching position at the conservatory in January of 1990, I finally shared the stage with Helmut Zacharias again. We had seen each other many times, but only at home with Hella and him in Ascona, where I am always welcome. We had not played together in public for decades. The Zweites Deutsche Fernsehen, the ZDF, (Second German Television Network) produced a film called *Ein Leben voll Musik* (A Life Full of Music) to celebrate his seventieth birthday. A bunch of his old friends, among them Paul Kuhn, Werner Müller, Margot Hielscher and Jean Toots Thielemans played a touching serenade to the young violinist. I was just a little disappointed that Helmut did not wear his old shepherd's checkered pants for the occasion . . . It was one of those evenings that makes your heart swell up until it feels like it's going to burst. It made us feel young again. Helmut and I even began to brainstorm about starting up new musical projects together.

Following the ZDF show, my quartet got a good reception at the Gostenhofener Jazz Days in Nuremberg, at the Berlin Jazztreff and at various small festivals. We recorded a couple of radio shows and participated in a few "historical" revues. We played once a month – and still do – at the old traditional Berlin club the *Ewige Lampe* on Leibnizstrasse, right in the middle of the quarter where it all began for me.

Sometimes I go for a walk down the streets and think about the many dimly-lit clubs, about the nights filled with music and the noise and smells that came out of the ventilators while I still did not know what was going on inside, in that big, big world. I think about Teddy Stauffer in front of the *Delphi*, and when I am at the Lietzenseepark, I think about the delicate balancing act I had to perform all those years ago in the snow. My relatives sit around me at the synagogue, and after the service, we go to see my grandparents and break matzo bread together after I mess up the prayer for the umpteenth time. A train rolls into the Halensee railroad station on its way to somewhere else, a freight train, and I peek through a crack in the door towards a house on Kronprinzendamm.

Auschwitz-Birkenau, I realized four years ago, smells like burning fat to everyone who was imprisoned there, then as now – like death. The wind blows the ashes of those who came on an earlier train into your face. When the sun dawns and turns the morning to gray, you count the shadows of those who went into the electrified fence the night before because they knew they could never sleep again. Our barracks stand quietly next to each other, waiting for the new arrivals. They are clean and neat, tall blades of grass cover the mud below. But in the haunt of memory nobody comes away with dry feet. I stand at the main gate and see my colleagues all around me; we are playing *La Paloma*. I ask myself if the life I have lived afterwards was right the way it was. A futile question that has no answer. The sad eyes that know what is coming, that briefly look at us as they pass by, are there and will always be there. Just like the music.

Three years ago, I was at a spa in Bad Bevensen, sitting on a terrace of a restaurant one warm summer evening, watching a magnificent sunset and enjoying myself. A number of happy young people had gathered at a table next to mine. Not much later, as it so often happens in my life, we began to enjoy each other's company. We bantered back and forth, joking with each other. They invited me to join them at their table. I bought them one round of drinks after another. To make a long story short: it was a good evening. A party was going on across the street, and we grabbed a table there. The young people talked about a lot of interesting things, about their jobs, a woman journalist was among them and at least two of them were policemen. When the conversation turned from job-related stuff and current events to politics and became intimate – after all, we were "among ourselves" – I quietly stopped ordering new rounds of drinks for everyone. Even though they were still in a good mood, they became serious. Their voices took on a forced determination. They gave me a lecture about the "foreigner problem" in Germany, from the journalistic perspective, but also from the point of view of the police. About the fact that there's a *Reinheitsgebot* (decree governing water purity) for beer but there isn't anything like that for the people's people anymore, about the fact that we're having trouble with world Jewry again and there must be some way to get a handle on these problems. Then the conversation turned to the "old fairytale" about the concentration camps, the gas and the ovens. After all, any halfway clever child knows by now that Auschwitz was one big lie.

The friends raised their glasses, the merry-go-round cast a kaleidoscope of multicolored lights on us as it whirled around. I did not know what I should do or say. Some time earlier, after the film by Paul Karalus about the death camps had been aired on TV and after all the interviews with me that followed in various newspapers, I found a postcard in my mailbox that showed two chimpanzees chasing each other. The anonymous greeting said "Jew, stop spreading your lies or you won't ever play in a ghetto orchestra again because the *Sturmscharen* (storm troopers) of the eastern Mark will get you!" There were any number of anonymous phone calls from people who told me I was a "Jew pig" and that they knew how to set my house on fire. I considered reporting the incidents

"As long as I make music I have no time to grow old."
Old Chinese proverb by Coco Schumann

to the police, but in the end I did not care to entrust my problems to them. It had been only a feeling then, but now I sat at a table with law and order types who wanted to demonstrate to me, an old gentleman, that there was hope for a "correct view" and that young people will think for themselves again by using worn-out slogans to question the truth about Auschwitz.

I interrupted the man sitting next to me in the middle of his sentence I did not care to follow, put my glass on the table, looked around at everyone and said: "Ladies and gentlemen, I am terribly sorry, I do not want to spoil your evening. But I know better than you. I was there." I did not wait for their reaction. I turned around and walked away, strolling through the city at night, whistling away to myself:

I got rhythm, I got music.
I got my girl – Who could ask for anything more?
I got daises in green pastures.
I got my girl – Who could ask for anything more!
Old Man Trouble, I don't mind him:
You won't find him, 'round my door!
I got rhythm, I got music.
I got my girl – Who could ask for anything more!

Afterword

BY MICHAEL H. KATER

I N THE LATE 1980s, I conducted research for a book on jazz in the
Third Reich. At first glance, the topic seemed absurd, for it was obvious
that the two represented opposites: jazz stood for individual freedom of
expression and the artistic avant-garde, National Socialism stood for oppression and cultural reaction. But after intensive work in archives and interviews
with contemporary witnesses, I found the two extremes to be both relevant and
real; where jazz had existed in Nazi Germany, there was a record of it being
suppressed, and there was a human story in the background that needed to be
told. Furthermore, and bizarrely, I found that the Nazis thought nothing of
using jazz for their own devious purposes, ideally to mold seductive propaganda
toward the enemy.

After having exhausted the archival records, I began interviewing
participants in the Weimar and Nazi German jazz scene for my book *Different
Drummers: Jazz in the Culture of Nazi Germany* (published in 1992 by Oxford
University Press) – musicians and aficionados who were now getting on in
age, living out their lives in the Federal Republic of Germany, Austria and
Switzerland, the United Kingdom and North America. I traveled everywhere
to visit them. Because I had myself performed in jazz formations earlier in my
life, I was credible to them; in one or two instances I even played with musicians
who were still active, as in the case of tenor saxophonist Emil Mangelsdorff. It
helped that I could converse with these survivors both in terms of music and
the political circumstances in which they themselves had once created music or
listened to it.

I enjoyed conducting the interviews with people who looked back at a time
when they were once younger than I was and who, as I found out, had lived

their passion at considerable risk to their own lives. Probably the most touching and in many ways the most incredible story I heard was from Coco Schumann in Berlin, who was living in a modest apartment with his wife, Gertraud, after having survived the concentration camps of Theresienstadt and Auschwitz. Schumann, who was still playing in Berlin clubs, struck me as a man with the kind of self-assured personality that inspires a will to live, to survive, a will not to succumb even in a hellhole such as Auschwitz. Schumann's life then, and his life now, both as a person and an artist, validated my earlier assumption that the book I was planning to write could be an important testament. A testament in support of jazz as an art form that defied a totalitarian regime successfully, and a testament for young men and women such as the young Coco who had the strength to make this happen.

When Coco Schumann entered the Berlin jazz scene in the 1940s as a teenager, he embarked on an aesthetic and a moral risk. Had he not had any Jewish parents, he should have been a member of the state-monopolist Hitler Youth which, in so many ways, he had reason to envy. They enjoyed privileges reserved only for purely "Aryan" youths, who were compelled by a law of March 1939 to join the organization from ages ten to eighteen. The Hitler Youth's culture for the boys (girls were groomed for a life of wife and motherhood) was determined by a military code of competition. After school and on weekends, there were exercise routines and drills, with boys attending in black-and-khaki uniforms. All manner of sports were at the top of the agenda, and especially expensive and normally prohibitive pastimes, such as motorcycling and gliding, were sought after. There were fencing, swimming, calisthenics, spear throwing, and ball games, including of course soccer, all of which were said to foster a mutual feeling of community. According to the Social Darwinian principles which governed Nazi dogma, the fittest and most daring boys were sought, for instance by forced tests of courage, such as making youths jump from five-meter boards into water, often when they could not swim. Others had to climb up the sides of ravines without proper support. These activities created a sense of exclusivity which in turn generated peer-group spirit – outside peer pressure made many children want to join before they were even eligible.

Among Hitler Youth activities, those of the music division may be singled out. These were determined less by individual than by collective performances, for instance in choirs, where also the girls could join in. Often music cadres were attached to a radio station, where Hitler Youth choirs or small orchestral ensembles broadcast live from studios. These groups also performed at public recitals, with politics never absent; at drill time the repetitious use of a song helped in the shaping of young minds, as part of the Nazi educational canon. The texts of songs often were ideologically charged. Some songs that were chanted in unison bore an explicitly martial character, with references to the German fatherland, duty, honor, blood and soil, culminating in fighting and death. One telling example of this was the song *Our Flag Is Showing Us the Way*, with lyrics by the would-be-poet von Schirach, used as early as 1933 in a Ufa film, *Hitlerjunge Quex*, which glorified the 1932 Nazi martyrdom of the early Hitler Youth Herbert Norkus. The song conjured up a battleground, spoke of defying danger, of a glowing Germany, of possible doom, of Adolf Hitler the Führer ("We are marching for Hitler through night and dread/With the banner of youth for freedom and bread"), reassuring the enraptured singers that "we are the soldiers of the future". Someone of Coco's character and love for individualism and expression that jazz offers would probably not have enjoyed being a Hitler Youth for long.

The Hitler Youth was also immersed early and systematically in one of the mainstays of Nazi ideology, anti-Semitism. That Jews were evil and had to be removed from German society and culture was taught to them in pep talks, formal speeches by Nazi greats and hate literature of the most primitive but effective kind. In Leni Reifenstahl's film about the 1934 Nuremberg Party Rally, *Triumph of the Will*, scores of Hitler Youths can be seen, whose privilege it had been to be sent there from all parts of Germany. The film audience is being informed where they came from: the Rhineland, Saxony, Mecklenburg, Hamburg – no territory is left out. Sixty-thousand youths camped on Rally ground and listened to official speakers, including Hitler, who extolled for them the superiority of the Germanic race, denigrating, even by implication, anything Jewish. In May 1938, Reich Economics Minister Walther Funk explained to his visiting Hitler Youth charges at a meeting in Berlin why all German Jews had to be expropriated. After taking from Jews their businesses and their wealth, Funk declared, one could grant them a kind of inferior leaseholder status, "so long as we do not have the capability to move them completely out of Germany". In the early 1940s, Hitler Youths were dispatched en masse to watch the film *Jud Süss* (Süss, the Jew), the most anti-Semitic feature film ever made in Nazi Germany. The youths learned their lessons. In Dresden in the early 1940s, when Jews were being rounded up for transport to Eastern ghettos and, eventually, liquidation camps, Hitler Youths eagerly officiated.

Both Adolf Hitler and his propaganda chief Joseph Goebbels had expressed a virulent anti-Semitism in the years before the Nazis took power in January 1933, Hitler in his book *Mein Kampf* and Goebbels in his diaries. But although Hitler had written that he wanted to destroy the Jews, few who read his book at the time took it seriously, least of all the Jews themselves. When the Nazis formed the government in late January 1933, most German citizens who were against them believed that the rule of Hitler and his henchmen would not last long. One of the first measures the new rulers undertook, however, was to boycott Jewish-owned shops and businesses, including cafés and nightclubs along Berlin's entertainment mile, where dance music and jazz were being played. In April, a law was promulgated ordering the dismissal of Jewish civil servants almost instantly throughout the land, and consequently, many non-state-employed Jews were also fired. Jewish physicians and lawyers had to close their offices to non-Jews. And in Berlin and elsewhere, many orchestras let their Jewish musicians go. Some of those were not German citizens, so it was even easier to dismiss them.

Yet another blow came to the Jews of Germany when, in September 1935, the so-called Nuremberg Laws were issued. Because there had been some uncertainty, the Nazis attempted to define who was a Jew. Paying no heed to current religious beliefs, they decided that anyone with three Jewish grandparents was to be regarded as fully Jewish, and as a result, pressure was applied to them to leave Germany, even if they were citizens. Formal citizenship for them, in fact, was revoked. Many German Jews, including artists, left Germany thereafter, most of them for the United States and Britain and some, who were Zionists, for the British mandate of Palestine. Others went to Austria, France, the Netherlands and Czechoslovakia, only to be caught again by the Nazis after they had invaded those countries. The famous actor Kurt Gerron, for instance, who had played Tiger Brown in Bertolt Brecht and Kurt Weill's original production of the *Threepenny Opera* in 1928, fled to Holland, whence the occupying Nazis deported him in early 1944 to Theresienstadt, the concentration camp in Terezín, Czechoslovakia, where he met Coco Schumann.

By the regulations of 1935, Schumann should have been classified as a half-Jew, because his father had not been Jewish; but because his mother had been, the Nazis applied Old Testament law declaring him a full Jew. By the Nuremberg race legislation, people with two Jewish grandparents were defined as *Mischlinge* of the first degree, whereas those with one were called *Mischlinge* of the second degree. The former group had less pressure applied to them to leave Germany and suffered fewer indignities than full Jews, some even serving in the armed forces and later doing forced labor; the last-mentioned group, for all intents and purposes could be regarded as ordinary Germans, but if they aroused suspicion, could be treated as Jews. The composer Carl Orff, who had a Jewish grandparent, hid this fact and behaved himself well, rising to the top of the Nazi artistic elite, while the Heidelberg professor of German literature Richard Alewyn, with similar parentage, had to leave the country as early as 1933.

During the violence of the Kristallnacht pogrom of November 1938 at the latest, it was clear to most German Jews that they should have left the Nazi Reich a long time ago. Yet then, when the Nazi doors were almost closed, there were too few foreign countries willing to grant would-be immigrants permission to enter. Many, like the United States and Australia, had national quotas, and the German one for 1938 was very quickly filled, whereas other countries, such as Canada, wanted no Jews at all. In fact, Canadian bureaucrats issued a motto to be followed in the processing of applications: "None is too many!" Emblematic is the story of the S.S. *St. Louis*; in May 1939, the ship tried to deliver German refugees with American visas to the United States via Cuba, was prevented by both countries from doing so and returned with its human cargo to Europe, where the majority of those passengers – mostly from Belgium – ultimately became victims of the Nazis.

By this time, in Germany, the remaining Jews were encouraged by the Third Reich leadership to join a Jewish Culture League, which had been set up in 1933 to accommodate the cultural needs of the Jews and sequester them more efficiently from the Germans. This was to be a Jewish culture vehicle staffed by Jews for Jews, to which ordinary Germans had no admittance. Many Jews welcomed this opportunity to play music, perform opera and plays and ballet, and even show some films, but the venture was closely controlled by the Gestapo. Goebbels, the propaganda minister, also used this *Kulturbund* for tight control over Jewish affairs. The slate of programs was limited; performing Mozart and Mendelssohn was permitted, Beethoven scarcely so, and Wagner and Richard Strauss not at all. With Kulturbund headquarters in Berlin, branches were established in many German cities and even smaller places such as Küstrin. There were several difficulties plaguing this venture over time, one being financial constraints, for the Jews had to finance everything themselves, and when opera, for instance, became too expensive to stage, it was abandoned. The Kulturbund also had a dance band, which made some records on its proprietary label, Lukraphon. Goebbels, who had staged Kristallnacht himself with the help of SS and SA men, used this control tool on the Jews ruthlessly, by applying and lifting prohibitions in short order. During Kristallnacht he commanded the Culture League to stop, only to force it open again a few days later; but nobody dared to attend. In the fall of 1941, the Kulturbund was ordered closed; by that time, Jews were being forbidden to leave the country. It was during 1941 that Berlin Jews were beginning to experience the first transports out of the capital to concentration camps and death camps.

In the German dance-band and jazz scene, the center of which was Berlin, there were therefore no Jews active by the mid-1930s and in the early 1940s, and very few partially Jewish musicians. One of those was the tenor saxophonist Eugen Henkel, who had two Jewish grandparents and who, before the war, impressed the visiting British bandleader Jack Hylton so much that he offered him a job. Another was the drummer Fritz Brocksieper, with one Jewish grandmother, who could play swing in a Benny Goodman mode, so that during the war he was assigned to the German-founded Charlie's Orchestra. The group performed in between propaganda harangues by the infamous Lord Haw-Haw, the renegade Briton William Joyce employed by Goebbels for broadcasts to the British Isles. (Despite fabulous drumming by Brocksieper, the British, and especially the soldiers, were not impressed, and after 1945 the phony lord was hanged at Wandsworth Prison.) Another, of course, was the young Coco Schumann.

Life was potentially even more dangerous for these jazz musicians than it was for the other, non-Jewish ones, for National Socialism defined jazz as the product of racially inferior Negroes and Jews. Still this did not mean that jazz, as it was traded on from the Weimar Republic into the Third Reich, was officially prohibited. In fact, until 1945, this was never the case. Jazz, imported to the Germany of the 1920s from America via Britain and France, had solidly established itself as a part of modernist Weimar culture, and especially in the large German centers like Berlin, Hamburg, Frankfurt and Munich, had a devoted following among the idle wealthy (think German Great Gatsbys), left-wing intellectuals and artists, and affluent youth. Key elements of it – rhythm, melody and harmony – had seeped into works by serious composers Ernst Krenek and Kurt Weill, and also into light-music compositions, including that of the society-dance culture and what on radio grew ever more into hit-parade-style music; hence jazz was a solid part of stage productions and popular culture in 1933 and beyond. Goebbels, as propaganda minister in charge of the direction of all culture in Nazi Germany, was careful to leave it alone. His aim was not to disturb the social peace among the populace; thus American-style jazz was featured in carefully designed broadcasts, and combos like The Golden Seven played in Berlin clubs such as *Moka Efti, Kakadu* or *Rosita Bar*. SS officers with exquisite if degenerate tastes were known to patronize such venues, while members of the Hitler Youth were kept away and exhorted, instead, to enjoy traditional German folk songs.

After the beginning of the war in September 1939, the German jazz scene tightened up. In his direction of culture for propaganda, Goebbels was now following a two-pronged policy. On the one hand, he wished to continue his indoctrination of the people to Nazify them further, culminating in their unquestioned acceptance of all of Hitler's racist and imperialist goals. This would include a strengthening of Nazi invective against Jews, the easier to get the German population to accept their continued disappearance from the streets. Toward this goal, for example, Goebbels had the anti-Semitic film *Jud Süss* shown to the public all over Germany in 1940, along with a contrived documentary entitled *Der ewige Jude* (The Eternal Jew), which was even more spiteful. (Many Germans embraced the first film, not least because of superior acting, but were repulsed by the second.)

However, Goebbels had to keep the civilian population in an emotional equilibrium, what with the deprivations of war, the shortage of foodstuffs and materials, increasing enemy bombings and the loss of men as soldiers at the fronts. For these purposes, high- and low-brow entertainment, in cinemas, in theaters, in the concert halls and in a few select big-city clubs, was important. In Berlin, only very few of the old clubs could hold their own, as musicians were conscripted into the Wehrmacht and air raids were making nightly outings hazardous for civilians. Jazz itself became a toxic medium after Germany had declared war on the United States in December 1941 and was being performed with ever increasing risk for the musicians.

It was in these circumstances that Coco Schumann, the guitarist, and Helmut Zacharias, his friend the violinist, both at the cusp of their twenties, were holding out, playing the swing they had heard on records and performed by older musicians, some now absent from Berlin. As a non-Jew, Zacharias had comparatively little to fear and, in between performances, was doing stints in the army, not least in order to protect himself. But to venture out and play publicly as he did, Coco Schumann was making both an aesthetic and a moral decision. Aesthetic because by devoting himself to jazz he knew that he was espousing an art form that was associated with the modernism of the republican era, yet also with America, all of which were anathema to the regime. And he committed himself to a moral choice because with his Jewish lineage, he was exposing his cultural heritage and ethnicity by embracing "Jewish" jazz. To have done both courageously as a teenager in such extremely dangerous times, without betraying his integrity, speaks volumes for him as an artist and a human being.

MICHAEL H. KATER, a former professional jazz musician, is Distinguished Research Professor of History Emeritus at York University in Toronto and a Fellow of the Royal Society of Canada. He is the author of eleven books, including *Hitler Youth* (Harvard 2004) and *Weimar: From Enlightenment to the Present* (Yale 2014). His latest will be *Culture in Nazi Germany*, which he is currently completing.

Coco Schumann: Discography
(SELECT)

Different spellings have been retained.

EDITOR'S NOTE: Songs with Coco Schumann's contributions have been singled out. Those designated as his compositions or arrangements are followed by his name in parentheses.

Nina Consta with the Helmut Zacharias Orchestra
Helmut Zacharias (vn), Hubertus Schulte (fl), Rudi Bohn (p), Hans Nowak (b), Nina Consta (v), Coco Schumann (g), among others
Berlin June 16, 1947
Odeon 0-26643: *Alta en el rancho grande* (High on the Big Ranch), *Ti-pi-tin*

Helmut Zacharias with the Berlin Allstar Band
(also known as Amiga-Star-Band)
Helmut Zacharias (vn), Hans Berry (tp), Mackie Kaspar (tp), Walter Dobschinski (tb), Omar Lamparter (cl), Detlev Lais (ts), Erwin Lehn (p), Coco Schumann (g), Teddy Lenz (b), Ilja Glusgal (dr)
Berlin May 21, 1948
Amiga Am 1150: *Honeysuckle Rose, Helmy's Be-bop Nr. 3*

Helmut Zacharias Quartet
Helmut Zacharias (vn), Rudi Balm (p), Klaus Dillmann (b), Coco Schumann (g)
Berlin July 9, 1948
Amiga Am 1151: *Schöner Gigolo, Helmy's Bebop #2*
Amiga Am 1152: *St. Louis Blues, Helmy's Bebop #1*
NOTE: All also listed under: Berlin May 21, 1948, with other title spellings:
Be-bop #1, St. Louis Blues, Be-bop #2, Just a Gigolo

Helmut Zacharias Quintet

Helmut Zacharias (vn), Rudi Bohn (p, harpsichord, organ), Coco Schumann (g), Klaus Dillmann (b), Kurt Grabert (dr, vib)

January 1949:

0Br ?: *Mr. Moneymaker* with Helga Wille and the Nicolets (v)

February 5, 1949:

Ich küsse ihre hand, Madame (I Kiss Your Hand, Madam); *Dark Eyes* (Br 82354)

Br 82360: *Those Little White Lies; Swing 4*

March 1949:

Br 82359: *Kosaken-Patrouille* (Cossack Patrol), (also Br 82424),

You Made Me Love You

Br 82364: *The Man I Love, Mob Mob, All on Pol* (*Alle auch auf Pol*) 2664 255 and BCD 15642

June 1949:

Br ?: *Whispering*

August 1949:

Br ?: *Twelve Street Rag, All on pol* (*Alle auch auf Pol*) 2664 255

Leo Rosner and his Gypsy Band

Homecraft Recordings, Australia; circa 1950

H-C 21001/2: *Russian Pot Pourri*

H-C 21003/4: *Hungarian Medl(e)y, Doina voda* (Romanian dance)

H-C 21005/6: *Tiomnaya notch* (Dark Night, tango), *Ogonek* (Girl's farewell to a soldier, tango)

H-C 21007/8: *La habanera, Oczy czornya* (Dark Eyes, Russian tango, sung by Peter Kotek, baritone)

H-C 21009/10: *Tabou* (slow rumba), *Bésame mucho* (sung in Polish by Peter Kotek)

H-C 210011/12: *Classic samba, Serce* (Heart, Russian tango, sung by Peter Kotek)

Coco Schumann's Quintet: Rhythm Cocktail

10", Spotlight Varieties S.V. 24, Thornbury/Melbourne, Australia; 1952

Always, Two Sleepy People, Minuet, Mean to Me, Sur le pont d'Avignon, Summertime, North West Passage, What Is This Thing Called Love

Geoff Kitchen's Quintet with Guitarist Coco Schumann: The Melody Lingers

10", Spotlight Varieties S.V. 25, Thornbury/Melbourne, Australia; circa 1950

(g, vib & p, acc, b, dr)

Get Happy, Music Maestro Please, You Came Along from Out of Nowhere,
Indian Summer, When I Take My Sugar to Tea, September in the Rain, On the
Sunny Side of the Street, This Song Is Ended

Coco Schumann and his soloists
Austroton Elite Special, 9389-45 (Single)
El Sombrero, Taverna del Corsare

Helmut Zacharias and his Swingtet: Swing is in
Helmut Zacharias (vn), Peter Jacques (vn), Coco Schumann (g), Mica Matejic (g),
Hans Rettenbacher (b), Meini Geppert (dr)
LP, EMI Electrola, HörZu I C 062-29 627; 1976
The Sheik of Araby, Mr. Paganini, Music Maestro Please, Honeysuckle Rose, Deep
Purple, Sweet Georgia Brown, Swing in Spring, You Made Me Love You, Jeepers
Creepers, Blues Intim (Intimate Blues), *When You Smile, Swing Is In*

Helmut Zacharias and his Swingtet: Swinging Christmas
Die schonsten Weihnachtslieder zum Tanzen (The Most Beautiful Christmas
dancing music)
Helmut Zacharias (vn), Peter Jacques (vn), Coco Schumann (g), Mica Matejic (g),
Hans Rettenbacher (b), Meini Geppert (dr)
LP, EMI Electrola I C 062-31 821
O Tannenbaum (Oh Christmastree), *Susser die Glocken* (Sweeter the Bells Have
Never Rung), *Eine Muh eine Mah (A Mood and a Baa), Am Weihnachtsbaume*
(Under the Christmas Trees), *Jingle Bells, Susanni –Susanni, Swinging Christmas,*
Ihr Kinderlein kommet (Come Hither Ye Children), *Leise rieselt der Schnee*
(Quietly Falls the Snow), *Kling Glockchen klingelingeling* (Ring Little Bell), *Morgen*
Kinder wirds was geben (Tomorrow Is What Children Give), *White Christmas*

Coco Schumann Quartet:
Coco Schumann live at the *Ewige Lampe*
Coco Schumann (g), Wolfgang Kohler (p), Micky Bahner (b), Horst Sommer (dr)
Live recording radio Bremen April 24, 1996
Publication as a compact cassette
Lester Leaps In, Just Friends, The Girl from Ipanema, Here Is That Rainy Day,
Let's Fall in Love, Autumn Leaves, Satin Doll, Stripper Blues (Coco Schumann),
Continental, Exotique (Coco Schumann), *Stompin' at the Savoy, Nuages, Blue*
Room, Coco Nuts (Coco Schumann)

Coco Schumann: Double, Fifty Years in Jazz
Double-album CD, Trikont US-0238; 1997
A cross-section of recordings of / with Coco Schumann

Coco Now! Coco Schumann Quartet Live
CD, Trikont US-0266 / LC4270; 1999
Coco Schumann (g), Karl-Heinz Böhm (ts, fl, v),
Hans Schätzke (b), Sven Kalis (dr)
Among others:
Stripper Blues (Coco Schumann)

Coco Schumann: Rex Casino, Munich: Three Continents
Trikont US 0381 CD + DVD; 2009
Coco Schumann's tape recording of his 1955 Rex Casino concert
DVD edited by Kalle Laar from Super-8 footage filmed by Coco Schumann in
Berlin, Beruit and Senegal

Coco Schumann:
Coco on vinyl – 90 Years in Jazz
CD, Trikont US-0466; May 16, 2014
Exotique 1963, Taverna del Corsare, Ausgerechnet heut abend (Just Tonight), *Sur le
pont, Mean to Me, There'll Never Be Another You, Westwind, Meine Gitarre erzählt*
(My Guitar Tells All), *Senorita de la mambo, Summertime, Stripper Blues, Here's That
Rainy Day*
(Coco Schumann)

Coco – Best of Coco Schumann
CD, C + P Trikont US-0466/LC 04270; 2014
Among others:
*Exotique 1963, Taverna del Corsare, Westwind, Meine Gitarre erzählt, Señorita de la
Mambo, Stripper Blues 1, Here's That Rainy Day*
(Coco Schumann)

COMMON INSTRUMENTS ARE ABBREVIATED AS:

b = bass	fl = flute	tp = trumpet	v = voice
cl = clarinet	g = guitar	tb = trombone	vib = vibraphone
dr = drums	p = piano	ts = tenor saxophone	vn = violin

Compilations

Helmi's Swing
Hot shots of the '40s with Halmut Zacharias and his soloists
EMI Electrola, The Golden Hopper
Historical photographs
DLPLC 0287, ICI34-45361/62N
Among others:
Nina Consta with the Helmut Zacharias Orchestra
Alla en el rancho grande, Ti-pi-tin (Odeon O-26643)
Helmut Zacharias Quartet
Helmy's Bebop #1, Helmy's Bebop #2, Schöner Gigolo (Beautiful Gigolo)*, St. Louis Blues*
Helmut Zacharias with the Berlin Allstar Band
Helmy's Bebop #3, Honeysuckle Rose

Jazz on Amiga 1947-1962, Vol. I
Amiga Mono 8 50 852; 1981
Among others:
Helmut Zacharias Quartet
Be-bop #1, St. Louis Blues, Be-bop #2, Just a Gigolo
Amiga-Star-Band
(Instrumentation identical to Berlin Allstar Band) *Helmy's Be-bop #3, Honeysuckle Rose*

My Gift to You
Philips mono P 48 100 L / stereo 840 478 PY
Among others:
Jean "Toots" Thielemans (harmonica), **Simon Krapp Orchestra**
Au revoir, mon amour (Good-bye, My Love) (Coco Schumann)

Midnight-Music
Austroton Elite Special SOLP 33-216
Among others:
Coco Schumann Combo
Taverne del Corsare, Senorita de La Mambo (Coco Schumann)

Helmut Zacharias Quartet: I have Rhythm
Original Brunswick/Polydor/Heliodor-images; 1949-1957
CD, Bear Family Records 513 966-2; BCD 15642 AH; 1992
(Contrary to the title of this CD, there are no recordings of HZ Quartet)
Among others:
Helmut Zacharias Quintet
Ich küsse Ihre Hand, Madame; Dark Eyes (Br 82354)
Those Little White Lies, Swing 48 (Br 82360)
Kosaken-Patrouille (Br 82359/82424)
You Made Me Love You (Br 82359)
The Man I Love, Mob Mob (Br 82364)

La Paloma – One song for all worlds Vol. 2
CD, Trikont US-0227 / LC 4270; 1996
Among others:
Coco Schumann Combo
Coco Schumann (g), Karl-Heinz Böhm (ts),
Niels Unbehagen (p), Thomas Fassnau (b),
Horst Sommer (dr)
La Paloma

Cover Versions
(SELECT)

The Rhythm Masters
Columbia stateside, C 22 343 / 45-DW 6090
Among others:
Exotique (Coco Schumann), 7 XCR 50169

Robert Mersey & His Orchestra
Columbia 4-42584
Among others:
Kookaburra (Coco Schumann), JZSP 57871

The Versatile Martin Denny
USA, Liberty Records Mono LRP-3307 / Stereo LST-7307
Exotique Bossa Nova (Coco Schumann)

Chronology of documentary films and television
featuring Coco Schumann
(SELECT)

Paul Karalus / Alfred Segeth:
Deutschlandbilder. Aus einem Musikerleben. Coco, der Ghetto-Swinger (German pictures. From a musician's life. Coco, the Ghetto-Swinger)
1986. Film, 45 min.

John Jeremy / Roy Ackermann:
Swing under the Swastika: The Story of a Music That Could Kill and Save
1990. Film (two-part documentary), 52 min.

Gabriele Deneke:
Tanz in den Abgrund. Das ungewöhnliche Leben des Jazzmusikers Coco Schumann (Dance into the abyss. The unusual life of a Jazz musician Coco Schumann)
1996. Film, 45 min.

Ilona Ziok:
Kurt Gerron's Karussell (Kurt Gerron's Carousel)
1999. Film, 70 min.

Reinhold Beckmann:
Beckmann (talk show)
1999. Television, one episode.

Tom Vogt:
Das Jahrhundert des Kabaretts (The Century of Cabarets)
2001. Television, one episode.

Malcolm Clarke / Stuart Sender:
Prisoner of Paradise
2002. Film, 96 min.

Mario Adorf / Coco Schumann:
Mein Kriegsende (My End-of-War)
2005. Television, one episode.

Julian Benedikt:
Play Your Own Thing: A Story of Jazz in Europe
2006. Film, 88 min.

Monica Ladurner / Wolfgang Beyer:
Schlurf: Im Swing Gegen den Gleichschritt (Schlurf: Swing against Lock-Step)
2007. Film, 71 min.
Note: In Austria, according to the film, "Schlurf" was the colloquial word youths
enamored of swing used to refer to themselves: "carelessly dressed, degenerate,
panderer…"

Sigrid Faltin / Makame Faki:
La Paloma. Sehnsucht. Weltweit. (La Paloma. Life's Longings, across the World)
2008. Film, 86 min.

Swantje Bahnsen / Birte Hoffmann / Katherina Lörsch / Luisa Martini / Alexandra
Peewa / Nina Rudolph:
In Full Swing: Swing in Berlin, damals und heute (Swing in Berlin, then and now)
2010/2011. Television, 30 min.

Andrea Roth:
Musik als zuflucht: Der Swing-Gitarrist Coco Schumann (Refuge in Music: The swing
guitarist Coco Schumann)
June 3, 2014. Television, 15 min.

Dorothee Binding / Benedict Mirow:
Musik als zuflucht – Terezín | Theresienstadt (Refuge in Music – Terezín |
Theresienstadt)
2014. Film, 60 min. plus 105 min. live concert.
N O T E : awarded the French "Diapason d'Or", the Luxembourg "Supersonic Award"
and the "International Classical Music Awards 2014" (ICMA) Best Documentary in
the field of classical music.

ZDF (Zweites Deutsches Fernsehen, German public television):
Aspekte – Mit musik das KZ überlebt: Coco-Schumann (He survived concentration
camps with music)
January 23, 2015. Television, one episode.

RBB (Rundfunk Berlin-Brandenburg, Berlin public television):
Thadeusz, talk show with Jörg Thadeusz
January 27, 2015. Television, one episode.

Chronology of stage productions and other select publications
about the life of Coco Schumann

The Ghetto Swinger, a stage production with Konstantin Moreth starring as Coco Schumann, written by Kai Ivo Baulitz, performed at the Renaissance Theater in Berlin, 2012.

I Got Rhythm: Das Leben der Jazzlengende Coco Schumann, a graphic novel by Caroline Gille and Niels Schröder, published by be.bra verlag, 2014.

COCO – so lange ich Musik mache – habe ich keine Zeit alt zu werden ("As long as I am making music I don't have time to grow old"), a CD compilation of Coco's music along with photographs, edited by Bärbel Petersen and published by Lichtig Verlag, Berlin, May 2014.

Wir waren Nachbarn (We were neighbors), an exhibition at the Schöneberg Berlin City Hall featuring Coco Schumann's music and an album of his photographs as part of a display with one hundred and forty-eight Jewish citizens of Berlin and their times and lives, Summer 2014.

Jazzlegende Coco Schumann: "Dass ich hier sitze, habe ich der Musik zu verdanken" ("The fact I'm sitting here, I owe to the music"), a feature article in *Der Spiegel* online by Katya Iken, January 18, 2015.

In March and April 2015, a new musical production of *The Ghetto Swinger* by Kai Ivo Baulitz directed by Gil Mehmert and starring Helen Schneider and Konstantin Moreth. Coco Schumann attended the sold-out premiere at the Hamburger Kammerspiele. The show toured several theaters in Germany.

Die letzten Zeugen (The Last Witness) with Susanne Beyer and Martin Doerry, reports from nineteen survivors at the anniversary of the liberation of Auschwitz. *Der Spiegel*, January 2015, Number 5/24, pages 50-69. Coco Schumann is on the cover of this magazine.

Awards

1989 Order of Merit, Federal Republic of Germany
2008 Order of Merit, City of Berlin
2015 Ehrenpreise, a lifetime achievement award from the German Record Critics Association

Acknowledgments

DoppelHouse Press and Coco Schumann would like to thank everyone who has contributed to the English translation of his memoirs and the production of this book, including the efforts of translator John Howard and advisor Karin Howard; Bärbel Peterson; editors Luke Currim, Carrie Paterson, Ellie Shoja and Jonee Tiedemann; book designer Curt Carpenter; Michael H. Kater; Dr. Karel Margry; archivists Bettina Ehrlenkamp at Deutsche FotoThek, Svenja Kaspar at the Deutsches Historisches Museum, Nathalie Minart at the Paris Police Archives, Emanuel Saunders at Yad Vashem, Martina Šiknerová at the Terezín Memorial, Aileen Tomzek at the Landesarchiv Berlin, and Caroline Waddell Koehler at the United States Holocaust Memorial Museum; Zuzana Dvořáková; Eva Mair-Holmes from Trikont Records; Horst Papeler-Dütsch from Proton Berlin; cover designer Kourosh Beigpour; and his publisher's representative Constanze Chory at Deutscher Taschenbuch Verlag.

Index

Coco Schumann is denoted by CS and Gertraud Goldschmidt Schumann is denoted by GG. Photographs are indicated by page numbers in *italics*.

Coco Schumann Quartet
    at Berlin Jazztreff, 142
    costume party on *Taras Shevchenko*, *122*
    as "German-Arab" band, 124
    at Gostenhofener Jazz Days, Nuremberg,
        142
    new quartet formed, 140
    postcard, *121*
Coco Schumann Quintet, 93, 94, 96
"coffin ship", 94
Colombo, Ceylon, at D. Andrews' club, 95
Commonwealth Jubilee, Canberra, Australia,
    89–90
Como, Perry, 119
concentration camps
    CS in as young man, 1
    Holocaust denial, 143
    revisiting memories, 138
    ten million deported to between 1933–1941,
        31
    See also individual camps
Constantinople, 6
Cramer, Susanne, 101
cruise ship gigs, 120–121, 128–129
custom guitar, 131
Czech dumplings at Theresienstadt, 40

D
Dachau concentration camp, 60
Daily Girl Club, 115
Dajos Béla dance orchestra, 6
Dean, James, 102
Delphi-Palast club, 15–16, 23, 92–93
deportations to concentration camps from
    Berlin, 31
Der Blaue Engel (The Blue Angel; film), 45, 75
Der ewige Jude (The Eternal Jew; film), 152
Der Führer schenkt den Juden eine Stadt (The
    Führer Gives a City to the Jews), as wrong
    title for Nazi film, 44
Der Ich-Du-Er-Sie-Eskimo (word play on pro-
    nouns; Glusgal), 84
Desmond, Paul, 114
Deutscher, Drafi, 111
DIAS. *See* RIAS (*Radio Im Amerikanischen
    Sector*)
Die Badewanne (The Bathtub) club, 98, 100,
    136
Die Drei von der Tankstelle (The Three from
    the Filling Station; film), 45
Die Philharmoniker (film), 33–34
Dietrich, Marlene, 45, 73–76, *74*
Different Drummers (Kater), 146
Dillman, Klaus, 81

Dischereit, Heinz, 98–99, 100
Dobberke, Walter, 36
Dobschinski, Walter, 96, 103
Dorette club, 17
D'Orio, Lubo, 96
Dosvedanje, 122
Downbeat! Big Band Bash, 93–94
Drei Travellers (Three Travelers), 76
Dreigroschenoper (The Threepenny Opera;
    Brecht and Weill), 44–45
Drugstore club, 112
dry cleaners/hair salon combination, 119

E
"*...endlich wieder Jazz im Sportpalast*" ("... Fi-
    nally – Jazz Returns to the *Sportpalast*"), 96
Egyptian secret police, 124
Eichmann, Adolf, 70, 108
Ein Leben voll Musik (A Life Full of Music;
    film), 142
Eine Nacht voller Seligkeit (A Night Full of
    Bliss), 57
electric guitars, 77
Ellington, Duke, 13, 106
emigration from Germany, difficulty finding
    accepting countries, 150
Endlösung der Judenfrage (Final Solution of the
    Jewish Question), 30, 108
Endsieg (final victory), 60
Enrico (Afro-Cuban band member), *103*
Ententanz (Dance of the Duck), 136
entertainment coupons, 39
Eppstein, Dr. (Jewish elder), 49
Erhard, Ludwig, 115
Erhardt, Heinz, 101
Erholung (Repose) club, Hamburg, 84
Ernst, Rudy
    on clarinet at Groschenkeller, *28*
    on clarinet at Wannaseebad, *27*
    with CS and Glusgal, *27*
    with CS at Rosita Bar, 24
    as *mampe* at Groschenkeller, 29–30
Es war einmal ein treuer Husar ... (Once There
    Was a Loyal Husar...), 98
Etzel, Roy, 108
Ewige Lampe (Eternal Lamp) club, 1, 142
Exotique (Schumann), 130

F
Fährenwald sickbay, 62
family religious dynamics, 4–5
family time, lack of, 105–106
Faun club, 128
Fender Guitar Company, 104

Kurz, Bud, 129

Coco Schumann (May 14, 1924–January 28, 2018) was an award-winning swing and jazz musician. A guitarist, drummer, band leader and composer, Schumann put out numerous record collections during his lifetime. His latest appeared in 2014, and until his retirement later that year at ninety years old, Schumann was playing regularly in Berlin for packed crowds. With many accolades to his name, Schumann was notably a recipient of Orders of Merit from both the city of Berlin (2008) and from the Federal Republic of Germany (1989) as well as having received the prestigious Ehrenpreis Lifetime Achievement Award from the German Record Critics in 2015. As one of the last witnesses of the Holocaust, Schumann's testimonial book is read widely in schools. A musical about his life played in Hamburg and Berlin in 2012 and 2018, and he has appeared in several documentary films. At the time of his death in Berlin at age 93, he was already a legend, considered one of Germany's greatest swing and jazz musicians.

CONTRIBUTOR BIOGRAPHIES

John Howard, an American who lived in Berlin for more than two decades, has translated books from German to English and edited and translated screenplays and treatments for film. He taught English language and literature in the U.S., Germany and Beijing and has been engaged as a producer-director for German radio and television (SWF, BR, HR). He is currently working on a book about his experiences living in China.

Michael H. Kater, a former professional jazz musician, is Distinguished Research Professor of History Emeritus at York University in Toronto and a Fellow of the Royal Society of Canada. He is the author of eleven books, including *Hitler Youth* (Harvard 2004) and *Weimar: From Enlightenment to the Present* (Yale 2014). His latest will be *Culture in Nazi Germany*, which he is currently completing.

Co-author **Michaela Haas** is a journalist and life coach as well as the author of several self-transformation books. She has written for Germany's leading newspapers and was the host of an award-winning TV interview program. She holds a PhD in Asian studies.

Co-author **Max Christian Graeff** is a German author and publisher. He has written several books and essay collections (in German) published by Deutsches Taschenbuch Verlag and NordPark Verlag, has made art, given performances and lectures and has sung with the German rock band The Morlocks.